Mother Courage

a chronicle play of the Thirty Years War, was
written in 1938–9 and first produced in Zürich
in 1941. Mother Courage follows the armies
with her travelling canteen, selling provisions
and liquor to the troops. She loses both her
sons in the war, and her dumb daughter
Kattrin is shot as she beats a drum to warn the
town of Halle of an impending attack. Mother
Courage is left alone with her wagon, old but
still business-like.

D1418958

*The photograph on the front of the cover shows
Helene Weigel as Mother Courage in the 1949
production of* Mother Courage and her Children
*at the Deutsches Theater, Berlin. Reproduced by
courtesy of The Berliner Ensemble. The photograph on the back is reproduced by courtesy of
Eric Bentley.*

Mother Courage
and her Children

A CHRONICLE
OF THE THIRTY YEARS WAR
BY
BERTOLT BRECHT

translated by Eric Bentley

LONDON
EYRE METHUEN LTD
11 NEW FETTER LANE EC4

All inquiries concerning the rights for
professional or amateur stage production should
be directed to the
International Copyright Bureau Ltd,
26 Charing Cross Road, London, WC2

First published 1962 *by Methuen & Co Ltd*
Seventh impression 1972
This translation copyright © 1955, 1959, 1961, 1962
by Eric Bentley;
original work published under the title of
MUTTER COURAGE UND IHRE KINDER
copyright 1949 *by Suhrkamp Verlag*
vormals S. Fischer, Frankfurt/Main
All rights reserved
Printed in Great Britain by
Cox & Wyman Ltd., Fakenham, Norfolk
SBN 416 63010 3

Preface

As we look back today upon the career of Bertolt Brecht (1898–1956) two periods of maximum creativity define themselves. The first came with the onset of manhood: Brecht had written some of his finest poetry, dramatic and otherwise, before he was twenty-five. The second came when he had perforce to withdraw from the hectic political activity of the Depression Years and lead the life of an exile during the later thirties and earlier forties. This is the period of *The Good Woman of Setzuan*, *The Life of Galileo Galilei*, *The Caucasian Chalk Circle*, and of what many regard as his masterpiece, *Mother Courage and her Children*.

In this play, and *Galileo*, Brecht withdrew, not only from Nazi Germany, but from the twentieth century, and it is not without interest that the century he took in exchange was, in both instances, the seventeenth. It is the century of greatness, a century that opens with William Shakespeare and closes with Isaac Newton. Brecht finds in that century the roots of his own philosophy of life, scientific humanism. 'Of all the days,' he writes of the day when Galileo had to decide whether to abjure Copernicus, 'that was the one / An age of reason could have begun.' This at any rate is the 'thesis' in the dialectical process: the 'antithesis' is represented by the Thirty Years War (1618–48).

For Germans, this is not 'just another war'. In the way it bore down upon whole cities and populations, it remained unique in German history until 1944–5. Since Brecht's play was finished before World War II began, this 'cross-reference' has a sadly prophetic character.

One wonders if some friend mailed Brecht a copy of an English book that came out the year before he wrote *Mother Courage*, namely, *The Thirty Years War* by C. V. Wedgwood. Here is Miss Wedgwood's summing-up:

After the expenditure of so much human life to so little purpose, men might have grasped the essential futility of putting the beliefs of the mind to the judgment of the sword. Instead, they rejected religion as an object to fight for and found others.

As there was no compulsion towards a conflict which, in despite of the apparent bitterness of the parties, took so long to engage and needed so much assiduous blowing to fan the flame, so no right was vindicated by its ragged end. The war solved no problem. Its effects, both immediate and indirect, were either negative or disastrous. Morally subversive, economically destructive, socially degrading, confused in its causes, devious in its course, futile in its result, it is the outstanding example in European history of meaningless conflict. The overwhelming majority in Europe, the overwhelming majority in Germany, wanted no war; powerless and voiceless, there was no need even to persuade them that they did. The decision was made without thought of them. Yet of those who, one by one, let themselves be drawn into the conflict, few were irresponsible and nearly all were genuinely anxious for an ultimate and better peace. Almost all – one excepts the King of Sweden – were actuated rather by fear than by lust of conquest or passion of faith. They wanted peace and they fought for thirty years to be sure of it. They did not learn then, and have not since, that war breeds only war.

Whether or not Brecht read Miss Wedgwood, there is an author we can be sure he did read: Hans Jacob Christoffel von Grimmelshausen (?1610–76), author of *The Life of the Arch-Imposter and Adventuress Courage*. Yet this work does not stand to *Mother Courage* as *The Beggar's Opera* stands to *The Threepenny Opera*. What Brecht took from Grimmelshausen was not a structure, nor yet a story, nor yet a protagonist. He took a name, and he took atmosphere. He entered Grimmelshausen's world and carried some of it away with him. He carried away, especially, Grimmelshausen's sense of death – death on a tremendous scale and all a result of man's inhumanity to man. A reader without German can check on this by dipping into the one Grimmelshausen work which has been translated into English, *The Adventures of a Simpleton* (Four Square Classics, New English Library Ltd, London).

Mother Courage and her Children is coming to be accepted universally as one of the important plays of the past quarter century. Critics in the East wish it had an optimistic ending, and critics in the West wish it was a traditional tragedy; which is to say that it is a play that both parties worry over, and which neither can get around.

'Pessimistic' or 'untragic' as he may be, Brecht has put his finger on what Sir Herbert Read has shrewdly called 'the problem of our age':

> The problem of our age is not a problem of conscience or commitment – of why people choose to die in wars for or against communism or fascism. The problem is rather why people who have no personal convictions of any kind allow themselves to suffer for indefinite or undefined causes, drifting like shoals of fish into invisible nets. The problem is mass-suffering, mute and absurd. . . .

Oddly enough, this quotation is taken from a passage in which Sir Herbert is complaining of the absence of tragic poetry in our day:

> We live in a tragic age, but we are unable to express ourselves in tragic poetry. We are inarticulate and our only art is mockery or self-pity. Our fatalism gives us a stoical appearance, but it is not a genuine stoicism. It is a dull animal endurance of misfortune, unfocussed and unexpressed. . . . There seems to be a direct connection between our inarticulateness, which implies a lack of emotional purgation, and our readiness to respond to mass appeals. Modern war in all its destructiveness is a dumb acceptance of this anonymous fate. Our armies, as Matthew Arnold said, are ignorant and clash by night.

But supposing this dull animal endurance, this inarticulateness, this dumb acceptance of anonymous fate is precisely the subject? Suppose the writer is not lost in it but sees it? Suppose he himself is not 'ignorant', but can show the 'clash by night' in a flood of lights? We might still conclude that Brecht has not achieved tragedy (that is a matter of semantics) but we shall begin to see the point of his whole approach. It is because he is not identified with Mother Courage as academicians, East or West, want him to be, that he does not fall into the trap Sir Herbert mentions, the trap of self-pity. 'Our only art is mockery or self-pity.' There is plenty of mockery in *Mother Courage*, but surely it is not such defensive irony as Sir Herbert presumably had in mind? This mockery helps to *dispel* self-pity.

It also includes a robust humour through which the prot-agonist ceases to be 'average' in the usual modern sense – a sort of lowest common factor, the human animal seen abstractly, as in public opinion surveys – and becomes someone who, how-ever lacking in the attributes of saint or heroine, is every inch a person.

When *Death of a Salesman* came out, there were discussions as to whether the story of such a 'little man' as Willie Loman (low man) could be regarded as tragic. If not, it was implied, then the poor chap would be left all alone with his littleness in outer darkness. About Mother Courage, one need have no such worries. Brecht need not rise up, like Arthur Miller, to broaden the theory of tragedy lest his protagonist be left out of things. Not being the abstract 'little man', Mother Courage can stand the outer darkness. She may even light it up. She represents, one might say, an alternative to tragedy.

But she does not represent Marxist optimism except when a director – as in Moscow, 1960, I believe – changes the ending and has her become a pacifist. Of traditional tragedy, *Mother Courage and her Children* retains the sense of overriding fate, the sheer inevitability. Is this pessimism? That, too, is a matter of semantics. I think it makes good sense to say, No, and again to claim that Brecht's work comes as an answer to a problem formulated by Sir Herbert Read. 'Or fatalism gives us a stoical appearance, but it is not a genuine stoicism.' Mother Courage doesn't present a stoical appearance, but I think she does embody a genuine stoicism. Though her name is an irony, and she is, in the first instance, a coward, she also, in the last analysis, needs courage – needs it merely to continue, merely to exist, and this courage is there – inside her – when she looks for it. A human being, she has human resources.

To clinch the point one need only ask oneself what a naturalistic playwright would do with Mother Courage at the end of his play. Would he not kill her off, probably by her own hand? How grotesque this 'solution' seems to anyone who has inhabited the world of Brecht's drama. Cannot Mother Courage say, with the same good right as the aristocratic Rilke: 'Wer spricht von Siegen? Überstehn ist alles': 'Who talks of victories? To see it through is everything'?

E.B.

Note

Mother Courage and her Children was copyrighted in the U.S.A.
in 1940, and first published there, not in German, but in English,
in 1941: the translation was by H. R. Hays, and the play
appeared in an anthology of new writing entitled *New Directions
1941*; and was published by New Directions. The world
première of the play (and this *was* in German) also took place in
1941 at the Zürich Schauspielhaus; the director was Leopold
Lindtberg.

The now famous production of the Berlin Ensemble dates
back to 1949 (though the Ensemble did not yet exist) when
Erich Engel and Bertolt Brecht put the play on at the Deutsches
Theater in Berlin with Helene Weigel (Mrs Bertolt Brecht) in
the title role. Frau Weigel is today (1962) one of the few actors
from the original cast who are still in the show.

Translated by Eric Bentley, *Mother Courage and her Children*
has been professionally staged in London, Bristol, Dublin,
Cleveland (Ohio), and San Francisco (California). It has also
been presented by BBC-TV.

The music to the world première in Zürich was by Paul
Burkhard, and there is also an as yet unused score by Darius
Milhaud, but the music generally associated with the play is
that of Paul Dessau. Part of Dessau's score can be heard, with
the words in French, on a Vanguard Record (VRS-9022); part
with the words sung in German by the Berlin cast, on East
German records usually available from Deutsche Schallplatten,
Deutscher Buch Export, Lenin-strasse 16, Leipzig C.1.

E.B.

Mother Courage and her Children

MUSIC: Paul Burkhard, Paul Dessau, Darius Milhaud

TRANSLATOR: Eric Bentley

Written 1936–9. First produced in the Zürich Schauspielhaus
on 19 April 1941

CHARACTERS

*Mother Courage : Kattrin, her dumb daughter : Eilif, her elder son :
Swiss Cheese, her younger son : the recruiting officer : the sergeant :
the cook : the Swedish commander : the chaplain : the ordnance
officer : Yvette Pottier : the man with the bandage : another sergeant : an old colonel : a clerk : a young soldier : an older soldier :
a peasant : a peasant woman : the young man : the old woman :
another peasant : the peasant woman : a young peasant : the
lieutenant : a voice.*

SPRING, 1624. IN DALARNA, THE SWEDISH COMMANDER
OXENSTIERNA IS RECRUITING FOR THE CAMPAIGN IN POLAND.
THE CANTEEN WOMAN ANNA FIERLING, COMMONLY KNOWN
AS MOTHER COURAGE, LOSES A SON

Highway outside a Town

A sergeant and a recruiting officer stand shivering.

Q 1.

Wind.

THE RECRUITING OFFICER: How the hell can you line up a company in a place like this? You know what I keep thinking about, Sergeant? Suicide. I'm supposed to knock four platoons together by the twelfth – four platoons the Chief's asking for! And they're so friendly round here, I'm scared to go to sleep at night. Suppose I do get my hands on some character and squint at him so I don't notice he's pigeon-chested and has varicose veins. I get him drunk and relaxed, he signs on the dotted line. I pay for the drinks, he steps outside for a minute, I have a hunch I should follow him to the door, and am I right? Away he's gone like a louse from a scratch. You can't take a man's word any more, Sergeant. There's no loyalty left in the world, no trust, no faith, no sense of honour. I'm losing my confidence in mankind, Sergeant.

THE SERGEANT: What they could do with round here is a good war. What else can you expect with peace running wild all over the place? You know what the trouble with peace is? No organization. And when do you get organization? In a war. Peace is one big waste of equipment. Anything goes, no one gives a damn. See the way they eat? Cheese on pumpernickel, bacon on the cheese? Disgusting! How many horses have they got in this town? How many young men? Nobody knows! They haven't bothered to count 'em! That's peace for you! I've been in places where they haven't had a war for seventy years and you know what? The people haven't even

3

been given names! They don't know who they are! It takes
a war to fix that. In a war, everyone registers, everyone's
name's on a list. Their shoes are stacked, their corn's in the
bag, you count it all up – cattle, men, *Et cetera* – and you
take it away! That's the story: no organization, no war!

THE RECRUITING OFFICER: It's God's truth, you know.

THE SERGEANT: Of course, a war's like any good deal: hard to
get going. But when it does get moving, it's a winner, and
they're all scared of peace, like a dice-player who daren't stop
– 'cause when peace comes they have to pay up. Of course,
until it gets going, they're just as scared of war, it's such a
novelty!

THE RECRUITING OFFICER: Hey, look, here's a canteen wagon.
Two women and a couple of young lads. Stop the old lady,
Sergeant. And if there's nothing doing this time, you won't
catch me freezing my arse in the April wind a minute longer.

(PROLOGUE)

*A harmonica is heard. A canteen wagon rolls on, drawn by two young
fellows. Mother Courage is sitting on it with her dumb daughter,
Kattrin.*

MOTHER COURAGE: A good day to you, Sergeant!

THE SERGEANT, *barring the way*: Good day to *you*! Who d'you
think *you* are?

MOTHER COURAGE: Tradespeople.

She sings:

> Here's Mother Courage and her wagon!
> Hey, Captain, let them come and buy!
> Beer by the keg! Wine by the flagon!
> Let your men drink before they die!
> Sabres and swords are hard to swallow:
> First you must give them beer to drink.
> Then they can face what is to follow –
> But let 'em swim before they sink!
>
> > Christians, awake! The winter's gone!
> > The snows depart, the dead sleep on.
> > And though you may not long survive
> > Get out of bed and look alive!

Your men will march till they are dead, sir.
But cannot fight unless they eat.
The blood they spill for you is red, sir.
What fires that blood is my red meat.
For meat and soup and jam and jelly
In this old cart of mine are found:
So fill the hole up in your belly
Before you fill one underground.

>Christians, awake! The winter's gone!
>The snows depart, the dead sleep on.
>And though you may not long survive
>Get out of bed and look alive!

THE SERGEANT: Halt! Where are you from, riff-raff?

EILIF: Second Finnish Regiment!

THE SERGEANT: Where are your papers?

MOTHER COURAGE: Papers?

SWISS CHEESE: But this is Mother Courage!

THE SERGEANT: Never heard of her. Where'd she get a name like that?

MOTHER COURAGE: They call me Mother Courage 'cause I was afraid I'd be ruined. So I drove through the bombardment of Riga like a madwoman, with fifty loaves of bread in my cart. They were going mouldy, I couldn't please myself.

THE SERGEANT: No funny business! Where are your papers?

MOTHER COURAGE *rummages among papers in a tin box and clambers down from her wagon*: Here, Sergeant! Here's a Bible – I got it in Altötting to wrap my cucumbers in. Here's a map of Moravia – God knows if I'll ever get there – the birds can have it if I don't. And here's a document saying my horse hasn't got foot and mouth disease – pity he died on us, he cost fifteen gilders, thank God I didn't pay it. Is that enough paper?

THE SERGEANT: Are you pulling my leg? Well, you've got another guess coming. You need a licence and you know it.

MOTHER COURAGE: Show a little respect for a lady and don't go telling these grown children of mine I'm pulling anything of yours. What would I want with you? My licence in the Second Protestant Regiment is an honest face. If *you* wouldn't know how to read it, that's not my fault, I want no rubber stamp on it anyhow.

THE RECRUITING OFFICER: Sergeant, we have a case of insubordination on our hands. Do you know what we need in the army? Discipline!

MOTHER COURAGE: I was going to say sausages.

THE SERGEANT: Name?

MOTHER COURAGE: Anna Fierling.

THE SERGEANT: So you're all Fierlings.

MOTHER COURAGE: I was talking about me.

THE SERGEANT: And I was talking about your children.

MOTHER COURAGE: Must they all have the same name? *Pointing to the elder son:* This fellow, for instance, I call him Eilif Noyocki – he got the name from his father who told me he was called Koyocki. Or was it Moyocki? Anyhow, the lad remembers him to this day. Only the man he remembers is someone else, a Frenchman with a pointed beard. But he certainly has his father's brains – that man could whip the breeches off a farmer's backside before he could turn round. So we all have our own names

THE SERGEANT: You're all called something different?

MOTHER COURAGE: Are you trying to make out you don't understand?

THE SERGEANT, *pointing at the younger son*: He's a Chinese, I suppose.

MOTHER COURAGE: Wrong again. Swiss.

THE SERGEANT: After the Frenchman?

MOTHER COURAGE: Frenchman? What Frenchman? Don't confuse the issue, Sergeant, or we'll be here all day. He's Swiss, but he happens to be called Feyos, a name that has nothing to do with his father, who was called something else – a military engineer, if you please, and a drunkard.

Swiss Cheese nods, beaming; even Kattrin smiles.

THE SERGEANT: Then how is it his name's Feyos?

6

MOTHER COURAGE: Oh, Sergeant, you have no imagination. *Of course* he's called Feyos: When he came, I was with a Hungarian. He didn't mind. He had a floating kidney, though he never touched a drop. He was a very *honest* man. The boy takes after him.

THE SERGEANT: But that wasn't his father!

MOTHER COURAGE: I said: he took after him. I call him Swiss Cheese. Why? Because he's good at pulling wagons. *Pointing to her daughter*: And that is Kattrin Haupt, she's half German.

THE SERGEANT: A nice family, I must say!

MOTHER COURAGE: And we've seen the whole wide world together – this wagonload and me.

THE SERGEANT: We'll need all that in writing. *He writes.* You're from Bamberg in Bavaria. What are you doing *here*?

MOTHER COURAGE: I can't wait till the war is good enough to come to Bamberg.

THE RECRUITING OFFICER: And you two oxen pull the cart. Jacob Ox and Esau Ox! D'you ever get out of harness?

EILIF: Mother! May I smack him in the kisser?

MOTHER COURAGE: You stay where you are. And now, gentlemen, what about a brace of pistols? Or a belt? Sergeant? Yours is worn clean through.

THE SERGEANT: It's something else *I'm* looking for. These lads of yours are straight as birch-trees, strong limbs, massive chests . . . What are such fine specimens doing out of the army?

MOTHER COURAGE, *quickly*: A soldier's life is not for sons of mine!

THE RECRUITING OFFICER: Why not? It means money. It means fame. Peddling shoes is woman's work. *To Eilif*: Step this way and let's see if that's muscle or chicken fat.

MOTHER COURAGE: It's chicken fat. Give him a good hard look, and he'll fall right over.

THE RECRUITING OFFICER: Yes, and kill a calf in the falling! *He tries to hustle Eilif away.*

MOTHER COURAGE: Let him alone! He's not for you!

THE RECRUITING OFFICER: He called my face a kisser. That is

an insult. The two of us will now go and settle the affair on the field of honour.

EILIF: Don't worry, Mother, I can handle him.

MOTHER COURAGE: Stay here. You're never happy till you're in a fight. He has a knife in his boot and he knows how to use it.

THE RECRUITING OFFICER: I'll draw it out of him like a milk tooth. Come on, young fellow-me-lad!

MOTHER COURAGE: Officer, I'll report you to the Colonel, and he'll throw you in gaol. His lieutenant is courting my daughter.

THE SERGEANT: Go easy. *To Mother Courage*: What have you got against the service, wasn't his own father a soldier? Didn't you say he died a soldier's death?

MOTHER COURAGE: This one's just a baby. You'll lead him like a lamb to the slaughter. I know you, you'll get five gilders for him.

THE RECRUITING OFFICER, *to Eilif*: First thing you know, you'll have a lovely camp and high boots, how about it?

EILIF: Not from you.

MOTHER COURAGE: 'Let you and me go fishing,' said the angler to the worm. *To Swiss Cheese*: Run and tell everybody they're trying to steal your brother! *She draws a knife.* Yes, just you try, and I'll cut you down like dogs! We sell cloth, we sell ham, we are peaceful people!

THE SERGEANT: You're peaceful all right: your knife proves that. Why, you should be ashamed of yourself. Give me that knife, you hag! You admit you live off the war, what else *could* you live off? Now tell me, how can we have a war without soldiers?

MOTHER COURAGE: Do they have to be mine?

THE SERGEANT: So that's the trouble. The war should swallow the peach-stone and spit out the peach, hm? Your brood should get fat off the war, but the poor war must ask nothing in return, it can look after itself, can it? Call yourself Mother Courage and then get scared of the war, your breadwinner? Your sons aren't scared, I know that much.

EILIF: Takes more than a war to scare me.

THE SERGEANT: Correct! Take me. The soldier's life hasn't done *me* any harm, has it? I enlisted at seventeen.

8

MOTHER COURAGE: You haven't reached seventy.

THE SERGEANT: I will, though.

MOTHER COURAGE: Above ground?

THE SERGEANT: Are you trying to rile me, telling me I'll die?

MOTHER COURAGE: Suppose it's the truth? Suppose I see it's your fate? Suppose I *know* you're just a corpse on furlough?

SWISS CHEESE: She can look into the future. Everyone says so.

THE RECRUITING OFFICER: Then by all means look into the sergeant's future. It might amuse him.

THE SERGEANT: I don't believe in that stuff.

MOTHER COURAGE: Helmet!

The sergeant gives her his helmet.

THE SERGEANT: It means less than a crap in the grass. Anything for a laugh.

MOTHER COURAGE *takes a sheet of parchment and tears it in two*: Eilif, Swiss Cheese, Kattrin! So shall we all be torn in two if we let ourselves get too deep into this war! *To the sergeant*: I'll give you the bargain rate, and do it free. Watch! Death is black, so I draw a black cross.

SWISS CHEESE: And the other she leaves blank, see?

MOTHER COURAGE: I fold them, put them in the helmet, and mix 'em up, the way all of us are mixed from our mother's womb on. Now draw!

The sergeant hesitates.

THE RECRUITING OFFICER, *to Eilif*: I don't take just anybody. I'm choosy. And you've got guts, I like that.

THE SERGEANT, *fishing around in the helmet*: It's silly. Means as much as blowing your nose.

SWISS CHEESE: The black cross! Oh, his number's up!

THE RECRUITING OFFICER: Don't let them get under your skin. There aren't enough bullets to go round.

THE SERGEANT, *hoarsely*: You cheated me!

MOTHER COURAGE: You cheated yourself the day you enlisted. And now we must drive on. There isn't a war every day in the week, we must get to work.

THE SERGEANT: Hell, you're not getting away with this! We're taking that bastard of yours with *us*!

EILIF: I'd like that, Mother.

MOTHER COURAGE: Quiet – you Finnish devil, you!

EILIF: And Swiss Cheese wants to be a soldier, too.

MOTHER COURAGE: That's news to me. I see I'll have to draw lots for all three of you. *She goes to the back to draw the crosses on bits of paper.*

THE RECRUITING OFFICER, *to Eilif*: People've been saying the Swedish soldier is religious. That kind of loose talk has hurt us a lot. One verse of a hymn every Sunday – and then only if you have a voice . . .

MOTHER COURAGE *returns with the slips and puts them in the sergeant's helmet*: So they'd desert their old mother, would they, the rascals? They take to war like a cat to cream. But I'll consult these slips, and they'll see the world's no promised land, with a 'Join up, son, you're officer material!' Sergeant, I'm afraid for them, very afraid they won't get through this war. They have terrible qualities, all three. *She holds the helmet out to Eilif*. There. Draw your lot. *Eilif fishes in the helmet, unfolds a slip. She snatches it from him.* There you have it: a cross. Unhappy mother that I am, rich only in a mother's sorrows! He dies. In the springtime of his life, he must go. If he's a soldier, he must bite the dust, that's clear. He's too brave, like his father. And if he doesn't use his head, he'll go the way of all flesh, the slip proves it. *Hectoring him*: Will you use your head?

EILIF: Why not?

MOTHER COURAGE: It's using your head to stay with your mother. And when they make fun of you and call you a chicken, just laugh.

THE RECRUITING SERGEANT: If you're going to wet your pants, I'll try your brother.

MOTHER COURAGE: I told you to laugh. Laugh! Now it's your turn, Swiss Cheese. You should be a better bet, you're honest. *He fishes in the helmet.* Oh dear, why are you giving that slip such a funny look? You've drawn a blank for sure. It can't be there's a cross on it. It can't be I'm going to lose *you*. *She takes the slip.* A cross? Him too! Could it be 'cause he's so simple-minded? Oh, Swiss Cheese, you'll be a goner too, if you aren't honest, honest, honest the whole time, the way I always brought you up to be, the way you always bring me all the change when you buy me a loaf. It's the only way you can save yourself. Look, Sergeant, if it isn't a black cross!

THE SERGEANT: It's a cross! I don't understand how *I* got one. I always stay well in the rear. *To the officer*: But it can't be a trick: it gets *her* children too.

SWISS CHEESE: It gets me too. But I don't accept it!

MOTHER COURAGE, *to Kattrin*: And now all I have left for certain is you, you're a cross in yourself, you have a good heart. *She holds the helmet up high towards the wagon but takes the slip out herself.* Oh, I could give up in despair! There must be some mistake, I didn't mix them right. Don't be too kind, Kattrin, just don't, there's a cross in your path too. Always be very quiet, it can't be hard since you're dumb. Well, so now you know, all of you: be careful, you'll need to be. Now let's climb on the wagon and move on. *She returns the helmet to the sergeant and climbs on the wagon.*

THE RECRUITING OFFICER, *to the sergeant*: Do something!

THE SERGEANT: I don't feel very well.

THE RECRUITING OFFICER: Maybe you caught a chill when you handed over your helmet in this wind. Get her involved in a business transaction! *Aloud*: That belt, Sergeant, you could at least take a look at it. These good people live by trade, don't they? Hey, all of you, the Sergeant wants to buy the belt!

MOTHER COURAGE: Half a gilder. A belt like that is worth two gilders. *She clambers down again from the wagon.*

THE SERGEANT: It isn't new. But there's too much wind here. I'll go and look at it behind the wagon. *He does so.*

MOTHER COURAGE: I don't find it windy.

THE SERGEANT: Maybe it's worth half a gilder at that. There's silver on it.

MOTHER COURAGE, *following him behind the wagon*: A solid six ounces worth!

THE RECRUITING OFFICER, *to Eilif*: And we can have a drink, just us men. I'll advance you some money to cover it. Let's go. *Eilif stands undecided.*

MOTHER COURAGE: Half a gilder, then.

THE SERGEANT: I don't understand it. I always stay in the rear. There's no safer spot for a sergeant to be. You can send the others on ahead in quest of fame. My appetite is ruined. I can tell you now: I won't be able to get anything down.

MOTHER COURAGE: You shouldn't take on so, just because you can't eat. Just stay in the rear. Here, take a slug of brandy, man. *She gives him brandy.*

THE RECRUITING OFFICER, *who has taken Eilif by the arm and is making off towards the back*: Ten gilders in advance and you're a soldier of the king and a stout fellow and the women will be mad about you. And you can give me a smack in the kisser for insulting you.

Both leave.
Dumb Kattrin jumps down from the wagon and lets out harsh cries.

MOTHER COURAGE: Coming, Kattrin, coming! The sergeant's just paying up. *She bites the half gilder.* I'm suspicious of all money, I've been badly burned, Sergeant. But this money's good. And now we'll be going. Where's Eilif?

SWISS CHEESE: Gone with the recruiting officer.

MOTHER COURAGE *stands quite still, then*: Oh, you simpleton! *To Kattrin*: You *can't* speak, I know. You are innocent.

THE SERGEANT: That's life, Mother Courage. Take a slug yourself, Mother. Being a soldier isn't the worst that could happen. You want to live off war and keep you and yours out of it, do you?

MOTHER COURAGE: You must help your brother now, Kattrin.

Brother and sister get into harness together and pull the wagon. Mother Courage walks at their side. The wagon gets under way.

THE SERGEANT. *looking after them:*
> When a war gives you all you earn
> One day it may claim something in return!

2

IN THE YEARS 1625 AND 1626 MOTHER COURAGE JOURNEYS
THROUGH POLAND IN THE BAGGAGE TRAIN OF THE SWEDISH
ARMY. SHE MEETS HER SON AGAIN BEFORE WALLHOF CASTLE. –
OF THE SUCCESSFUL SALE OF A CAPON AND GREAT DAYS FOR
THE BRAVE SON

Tent of the Swedish Commander   Q2. Cannon

*Kitchen next to it. Thunder of cannon. The cook is quarrelling with
Mother Courage, who is trying to sell him a capon.*

THE COOK: Sixty hellers for that paltry piece of poultry?

MOTHER COURAGE: Paltry poultry? Why, he's the fattest fowl
you ever saw! I see no reason why I shouldn't get sixty hellers
for him – this Commander can eat till the cows come home –
and woe betide you when there's nothing in your pantry . . .

THE COOK: They're ten hellers a dozen on every street corner.

MOTHER COURAGE: A capon like this on every street corner!
With a siege going on and people all skin and bones? Maybe
you can get a field rat! I said maybe. Because we're all out of
them too. Didn't you see the soldiers running five deep after
one hungry little field rat? All right then, in a siege, my price
for a giant capon is fifty hellers.

THE COOK: But we're not 'in a siege', we're doing the besieging,
it's the other side that's 'in a siege', when will you get this
into your head?

MOTHER COURAGE: A fat lot of difference that makes, *we* haven't
got a thing to eat either. They took everything in the town
with them before all this started, and now they've nothing to
do but eat and drink, I hear. It's us I'm worried about. Look
at the farmers round here, they haven't a thing.

THE COOK: Certainly they have. They hide it.

13

MOTHER COURAGE, *triumphant*: They have not! They're ruined, that's what. They're so hungry I've seen 'em digging up roots to eat. I could boil your leather belt and make their mouths water with it. That's how things are round here. And I'm expected to let a capon go for forty hellers!

THE COOK: Thirty. Not forty. I said thirty hellers.

MOTHER COURAGE: I say this is no ordinary capon. It was a talented animal, so I hear. It would only feed to music – one march in particular was its favourite. It was so intelligent it could count. Forty hellers is too much for all this? I know *your* problem: if you don't find something to eat and quick, the Chief will – cut – your – fat – head – off!

THE COOK: All right, just watch. *He takes a piece of beef and lays his knife on it.* Here's a piece of beef, I'm going to roast it. I give you one more chance.

MOTHER COURAGE: Roast it, go ahead, it's only one year old.

THE COOK: One *day* old! Yesterday it was a cow. I saw it running about.

MOTHER COURAGE: In that case it must have started stinking before it died.

THE COOK: I don't care if I have to cook it for five hours. We'll see if it's still hard after *that*. *He cuts into it.*

MOTHER COURAGE: Put plenty of pepper in, so the Commander won't smell the smell.

The Swedish Commander, a chaplain and Eilif enter the tent.

THE COMMANDER, *clapping Eilif on the shoulder*: In the Commander's tent with you my son! Sit at my right hand, you happy warrior! You've played a hero's part, you've served the Lord in his own Holy War, *that's* the thing! And you'll get a gold bracelet out of it when we take the town if *I* have any say in the matter! We come to save their souls and what do they do, the filthy, irreligious sons of bitches? Drive their cattle away from *us*, while they stuff their priests with beef at both ends! But you showed 'em. So here's a can of red wine for you, we'll drink together! *They do so.* The chaplain gets the dregs, he's pious. Now what would you like for dinner, my hearty?

EILIF: How about a slice of meat?

THE COMMANDER: Cook, meat!

THE COOK: Nothing to eat, so he brings company to eat it!

Mother Courage makes him stop talking; she wants to listen.

EILIF: Tires you out, skinning peasants. Gives you an appetite.

MOTHER COURAGE: Dear God, it's my Eilif!

THE COOK: Who?

MOTHER COURAGE: My eldest. It's two years since I saw him, he was stolen from me in the street. He must be in high favour if the Commander's invited him to dinner. And what do you have to eat? Nothing. You hear what the Commander's guest wants? Meat! Better take my advice, buy the capon. The price is one gilder.

THE COMMANDER, *who has sat down with Eilif and the chaplain, roaring*: Cook! Dinner, you pig, or I'll have your head!

THE COOK: This is blackmail. Give me the damn thing!

MOTHER COURAGE: Paltry poultry like this?

THE COOK: You were right. Give it here. It's highway robbery, fifty hellers.

MOTHER COURAGE: I said one gilder. Nothing's too high for my eldest, the Commander's guest of honour.

THE COOK, *giving her the money*: Well, you might at least pluck it till I have a fire going.

MOTHER COURAGE, *sitting down to pluck the capon*: I can't wait to see his face when he sees me. This is my brave and clever son. I have a stupid one as well but he's honest. The daughter is nothing. At least, she doesn't talk: we must be thankful for small mercies.

THE COMMANDER: Have another glass, my son, it's my favourite Falernian. There's only one cask left – two at the most – but it's worth it to meet a soldier that still believes in God! The shepherd of our flock here just looks on, he only preaches, he hasn't a clue how anything gets done. So now, Eilif, my son, give us the details: tell us how you fixed the peasants and grabbed the twenty bullocks. And let's hope they'll soon be here.

EILIF: In one day's time. Two at the most.

MOTHER COURAGE: Now that's considerate of Eilif – to bring the oxen tomorrow – otherwise my capon wouldn't have been so welcome today.

EILIF: Well, it was like this. I found out that the peasants had hidden their oxen and – on the sly and chiefly at night – had driven them into a certain wood. The people from the town were to pick them up there. I let them get their oxen in peace – they ought to know better than me where they are, I said to myself. Meanwhile I made my men crazy for meat. Their rations were short and I made sure they got shorter. Their mouths'd water at the sound of any word beginning with M, like mother.

THE COMMANDER: Smart fella.

EILIF: Not bad. The rest was a walkover. Only the peasants had clubs and outnumbered us three to one and made a murderous attack on us. Four of them drove me into a clump of trees, knocked my good sword from my hand, and yelled, 'Surrender!' What now, I said to myself, they'll make mincemeat of me.

THE COMMANDER: What did you do?

EILIF: I laughed.

THE COMMANDER: You what?

EILIF: I laughed. And so we got to talking. I came right down to business and said: 'Twenty gilders an ox is too much, I bid fifteen.' Like I wanted to buy. That foxed 'em. So while they were scratching their heads, I reached for my good sword and cut 'em to pieces. Necessity knows no law, huh?

THE COMMANDER: What do *you* say, shepherd of the flock?

THE CHAPLAIN: Strictly speaking, that saying is not in the Bible. Our Lord made five hundred loaves out of five so that no such necessity would arise. When he told men to love their neighbours, their bellies were full. Nowadays things are different.

THE COMMANDER, *laughing*: Quite different. A swallow of wine

16

for those wise words, you pharisee! *To Eilif*: You cut 'em to pieces in a good cause, our chaps were hungry and you gave 'em to eat. Doesn't it say in the Bible 'Whatsoever thou doest to the least of these my children, thou doest unto me?' And what *did* you do to 'em? You got 'em the best steak dinner they ever tasted. Mouldy bread is not what they're used to. They always ate white bread, and drank wine in their helmets, before going out to fight for God.

EILIF: I reached for my good sword and cut 'em to pieces.

THE COMMANDER: You have the makings of a Julius Caesar, why, you should be presented to the King!

EILIF: I've seen him – from a distance of course. He seemed to shed a light all around. I must try to be like him!

THE COMMANDER: I think you're succeeding, my boy! Oh, Eilif, you don't know how I value a brave soldier like you! I treat such a chap as my very own. *He takes him to the map.* Take a look at our position, Eilif, it isn't all it might be, is it?

MOTHER COURAGE, *who has been listening and is now plucking angrily at her capon*: He must be a very bad commander.

THE COOK: Just a greedy one. Why bad?

MOTHER COURAGE: Because he needs *brave* soldiers, that's why. If his plan of campaign was any good, why would he need *brave* soldiers, wouldn't plain, ordinary soldiers do? Whenever there are great virtues, it's a sure sign something's wrong.

THE COOK: You mean, it's a sure sign something's right.

MOTHER COURAGE: I mean what I say. Listen. When a general or a king is stupid and leads his soldiers into a trap, they need the virtue of courage. When he's tight-fisted and hasn't enough soldiers, the few he does have need the heroism of Hercules – another virtue. And if he's a sloven and doesn't give a damn about anything, they have to be as wise as serpents or they're finished. Loyalty's another virtue and you need plenty of it if the king's always asking too much of you. All virtues which a well-regulated country with a good king or a good general wouldn't need. In a good country virtues wouldn't be necessary. Everybody could be quite ordinary, middling, and, for all I care, cowards.

17

THE COMMANDER: I bet your father was a soldier.

EILIF: I've heard he was a great soldier. My mother warned me. I know a song about that.

THE COMMANDER: Sing it to us. *Roaring*: Bring that meat!

EILIF: It's called The Song of the Fishwife and the Soldier.

He sings and at the same time does a war dance with his sabre.

> To a soldier lad comes an old fishwife   Foldback
> And this old fishwife, says she:
> A gun will shoot, a knife will knife
> You will drown if you fall in the sea.
> Keep away from the ice if you want my advice
> Says the old fishwife, says she.
> But the soldier lad laughed and he loaded his gun
> And he reached for his knife and he started to run:
> It's the life of a hero for me!
> From the north to the south I shall march through the land
> With a knife at my side and a gun in my hand!
> Says the soldier lad, says he.
>
> When the lad defies the fishwife's cries
> The old fishwife, says she:
> The young are young, the old are wise
> You will drown if you fall in the sea.
> Don't ignore what I say or you'll rue it one day!
> Says the old fishwife, says she.
> But the soldier lad with his knife at his side
> And his gun in his hand steps into the tide:
> It's the life of a hero for me!
> When the new moon is shining on shingle roofs white
> We are all coming back, go and pray for that night!
> Says the soldier lad, says he.

MOTHER COURAGE *continues the song from her kitchen, beating on a pan with a spoon*:

> And the fishwife old does what she's told:
> Down upon her knees drops she.
> When the smoke is gone, the air is cold

Your heroic deeds won't warm me!
See the smoke, how it goes! May God scatter his foes!
Down upon her knees drops she.

EILIF: What's that?

MOTHER COURAGE, *singing on*:

But the soldier lad with his knife at his side
And his gun in his hand was swept out by the tide:
And he floats with the ice to the sea.
And the new moon is shining on shingle roofs white
But the lad and his laughter are lost in the night:
And he floats with the ice to the sea.

THE COMMANDER: What a kitchen I've got! There's no end to
the liberties they take!

EILIF *has entered the kitchen and embraced his mother*: To see
you again! Where are the others?

MOTHER COURAGE, *in his arms*: Happy as ducks in a pond. Swiss
Cheese is paymaster with the Second Regiment, so at least he
isn't in the fighting. I couldn't keep him out altogether.

EILIF: Are your feet holding up?

MOTHER COURAGE: I've a bit of trouble getting my shoes on in
the morning.

THE COMMANDER, *who has come over*: So, you're his mother!
I hope you have more sons for me like this chap.

EILIF: If I'm not the lucky one: you sit there in the kitchen and
hear your son being feasted!

MOTHER COURAGE: Yes. I heard all right. *She gives him a box on
the ear.*

EILIF, *his hand to his cheek*: Because I took the oxen?

MOTHER COURAGE: No. Because you didn't surrender when the
four peasants let fly at you and tried to make mincemeat of
you! Didn't I teach you to take care of yourself? You Finnish
devil, you!

The Commander and the chaplain stand laughing in the doorway.

3

THREE YEARS PASS AND MOTHER COURAGE, WITH PARTS OF A
FINNISH REGIMENT, IS TAKEN PRISONER, HER DAUGHTER IS
SAVED, HER WAGON LIKEWISE, BUT HER HONEST SON DIES.

A Camp

*The regimental flag is flying from a pole. Afternoon. All sorts of
wares hanging on the wagon. Mother Courage's clothes line is tied to
the wagon at one end, to a cannon at the other. She and Kattrin are
folding the washing on the cannon. At the same time she is bargaining
with an ordnance officer over a bag of bullets. Swiss Cheese, in paymaster's uniform now, looks on. Yvette Pottier, a very good-looking
young person, is sewing at a coloured hat, a glass of brandy before
her. She is in stocking feet. Her red boots are near by.*

THE OFFICER: I'm letting you have the bullets for two gilders.
Dirt cheap. 'Cause I need the money. The Colonel's been
drinking with the officers for three days and we've run out of
liquor.

MOTHER COURAGE: They're army property. If they find 'em on
me, I'll be courtmartialled. You sell your bullets, you bas-
tards, and send your men out to fight with nothing to shoot
with.

THE OFFICER: Oh, come on, if you scratch my back, I'll scratch
yours.

MOTHER COURAGE: I won't take army stuff. Not at *that* price.

THE OFFICER: You can resell 'em for five gilders, maybe eight,
to the Ordnance Officer of the Fourth Regiment. All you
have to do is to give him a receipt for twelve. He hasn't a
bullet left.

MOTHER COURAGE: Why don't you do it yourself?

THE OFFICER: I don't trust him. We're friends.

MOTHER COURAGE *takes the bag*: Give it here. *To Kattrin*: Take
it round the back and pay him a gilder and a half. *As the
officer protests*: I said a gilder and a half! *Kattrin drags the bag
away. The officer follows. Mother Courage speaks to Swiss
Cheese*: Here's your underwear back, take care of it; it's

October now, autumn may come at any time; I purposely don't say it must come, I've learnt from experience there's nothing that must come, not even the seasons. But your books *must* balance now you're the regimental paymaster. *Do* they balance?

SWISS CHEESE: Yes, Mother.

MOTHER COURAGE: Don't forget they made you paymaster because you're honest and so simple you'd never think of running off with the cash. Don't lose that underwear.

SWISS CHEESE: No, Mother. I'll put it under the mattress. *He starts to go.*

THE OFFICER: I'll go with you, paymaster.

MOTHER COURAGE: Don't teach him any hanky-panky.

Without a good-bye the officer leaves with Swiss Cheese.

YVETTE, *waving to him*: You might at least say good-bye!

MOTHER COURAGE *to Yvette*: I don't like that. *He's* no sort of company for my Swiss Cheese. But the war's not making a bad start. Before all the different countries get into it, four or five years'll have gone by like nothing. If I look ahead and make no mistakes, business will be good. Don't you know you shouldn't drink in the morning with your illness?

YVETTE: Who says I'm ill? That's libel!

MOTHER COURAGE: They all say so.

YVETTE: They're all liars. I'm desperate, Mother Courage. They all avoid me like a stinking fish. Because of those lies. So what am I arranging my hat for? *She throws it down.* That's why I drink in the morning. I never used to, it gives you crow's feet. But now it's all one, every man in the regiment knows me. I should have stayed at home when my first was unfaithful. But pride isn't for the likes of us, you eat dirt or down you go.

MOTHER COURAGE: Now don't you start again with your friend Peter and how it all happened – in front of my innocent daughter.

YVETTE: She's the one that should hear it. So she'll get hardened against love.

MOTHER COURAGE: That's something no one ever gets hardened against.

YVETTE: I'll tell you about it, and get it off my chest. I grew up in Flanders' fields, that's where it starts, or I'd never even have caught sight of him and I wouldn't be here in Poland today. He was an army cook, blond, a Dutchman, but thin. Kattrin, beware of thin men! I didn't. I didn't even know he'd had another girl before me and she called him Peter Piper because he never took his pipe out of his mouth the whole time, it meant so little to him.

She sings The Fraternization Song:

Foldback

Scarce seventeen was I when
The foe came to our land
And laid aside his sabre
And took me by the hand.
　　　And we performed by day
　　　The sacred rite of May
　　　And we performed by night
　　　Another sacred rite.
　　　The regiment, well exercised
　　　Presented arms, then stood at ease
　　　Then took us off behind the trees
　　　Where we fraternized.

Each of us had her foe and
A cook fell to my lot.
I hated him by daylight
But in the dark did not.
　　　So we perform by day
　　　The sacred rite of May
　　　And we perform by night
　　　That other sacred rite.
　　　The regiment, well exercised
　　　Presents its arms, then stands at ease
　　　Then takes us off behind the trees
　　　Where we fraternize.

Ecstasy filled my heart, O
My love seemed heaven-born!
But why were people saying
It was not love but scorn?
    The springtime's soft amour
    Through summer may endure
    But swiftly comes the fall
    And winter ends it all.
    December came. All of the men
    Filed past the trees where once we hid
    Then quickly marched away and did
    Not come back again.

I made the mistake of running after him, I never found him. It's ten years ago now. *With swaying gait she goes behind the wagon.*

MOTHER COURAGE: You've left your hat.

YVETTE: For the birds.

MOTHER COURAGE: Let this be a lesson to you, Kattrin, never start anything with a soldier. Love does seem heaven-born, so watch out! Even with those who're not in the army life's no honeypot. He tells you he'd like to kiss the ground under your feet – did you wash 'em yesterday, while we're on the subject? – and then if you don't look out, your number's up, you're his slave for life. Be glad you're dumb, Kattrin: you'll never contradict yourself, you'll never want to bite your tongue off because you spoke out of turn. Dumbness is a gift from God. Here comes the Commander's cook, what's bothering *him*?

Enter the cook and the chaplain.

THE CHAPLAIN: I bring a message from your son Eilif. The cook came with me. You've made, ahem, an impression on him.

THE COOK: I thought I'd get a little whiff of the balmy breeze.

MOTHER COURAGE: You're always welcome to that if you behave yourself, and even if you don't I think I can handle you. But what does Eilif want? I've no money to spare.

a   23

THE CHAPLAIN: Actually, I have something to tell his brother, the paymaster.

MOTHER COURAGE: He isn't here. And he isn't anywhere else either. He's not his brother's paymaster, and I won't have him led into temptation. Let Eilif try it on with someone else! *She takes money from the purse at her belt.* Give him this. It's a sin. He's speculating in mother love, he ought to be ashamed of himself.

THE COOK: Not for long. He has to go with his regiment now – to his death maybe. Send some more money, or you'll be sorry. You women are hard – and sorry afterwards. A glass of brandy wouldn't cost very much, but you refuse to provide it, and six feet under goes your man and you can't dig him up again.

THE CHAPLAIN: All very touching, my dear cook, but to fall in this war is not a misfortune, it's a blessing. This is a war of religion. Not just any old war but a special one, a religious one, and therefore pleasing unto God.

THE COOK: Correct. In one sense it's a war because there's fleecing, bribing, plundering, not to mention a little raping, but it's different from all other wars because it's a war of religion. That's clear. All the same, it makes you thirsty.

THE CHAPLAIN *to Mother Courage, pointing at the cook*: I tried to hold him off but he said you'd bewitched him. He dreams about you.

THE COOK, *lighting a clay pipe*: Brandy from the fair hand of a lady, that's for me. And don't embarrass me any more: the stories the chaplain was telling on the way over still have me blushing.

MOTHER COURAGE: A man of his cloth! I must get you both something to drink or you'll be making improper advances out of sheer boredom.

THE CHAPLAIN: That is indeed a temptation, said the court chaplain, and gave way to it. *Turning towards Kattrin as he walks*: And who is this captivating young person?

MOTHER COURAGE: She's not a captivating young person, she's a respectable young person.

24

*The chaplain and the cook go with Mother Courage behind the cart,
and one hears them talk politics.*

MOTHER COURAGE: The trouble here in Poland is that the Poles
would keep meddling. It's true our King moved in on them
with man, beast, and wagon, but instead of keeping the peace
the Poles were always meddling in their own affairs. They
attacked the Swedish King when he was in the act of peace-
fully withdrawing. So they were guilty of a breach of the
peace and their blood is on their own heads.

THE CHAPLAIN: Anyway, our King was thinking of nothing but
freedom. The Kaiser enslaved them all, Poles and Germans
alike, so our King *had* to liberate them.

THE COOK: Just what *I* think. Your health! Your brandy is first-
rate, I'm never mistaken in a face. *Kattrin looks after them,
leaves the washing, goes to the hat, picks it up, sits down,
and takes up the red boots.* And the war is a war of religion.
Singing while Kattrin puts the boots on: 'A mighty fortress is
our God . . .' *He sings a verse or so of Luther's hymn.* And
talking of King Gustavus, this freedom he tried to bring to
Germany cost him a pretty penny. Back in Sweden he had to
levy a salt tax, the poorer folks didn't like it a bit. Then, too,
he had to lock up the Germans and even cut their heads off,
they clung so to slavery and their Kaiser. Of course, if no one
had *wanted* to be free, the King wouldn't have had any fun.
First it was just Poland he tried to protect from bad men,
specially the Kaiser, then his appetite grew with eating, and
he ended up protecting Germany too. Now Germany put up
a pretty decent fight. So the good King had nothing but
worries in return for his outlay and his goodness, and of
course he had to get his money back with taxes, which made
bad blood, but he didn't shrink even from that. For he had
one thing in his favour anyway, God's Holy Word, which
was all to the good, because otherwise they could have said
he did it for himself or for profit. That's how he kept his
conscience clear. He always put conscience first.

MOTHER COURAGE: It's plain you're no Swede, or you'd speak
differently of the Hero King.

THE CHAPLAIN: What's more, you eat his bread.

THE COOK: I don't eat his bread. I bake his bread.

MOTHER COURAGE: He can never be conquered, and I'll tell you why: his men believe in him. *Earnestly*: To hear the big chaps talk, they wage war from fear of God and for all things bright and beautiful, but just look into it, and you'll see they're not so silly: they want a good profit out of it, or else the little chaps like you and me wouldn't back 'em up.

THE COOK: That's right.

THE CHAPLAIN: And as a Dutchman you'll do well to see which flag's flying here before you express an opinion!

MOTHER COURAGE: All good Protestants for ever!

THE COOK: A health!

Kattrin has begun to strut about with Yvette's hat on, copying Yvette's sexy walk. Suddenly cannon and shots. Drums. Mother Courage, the cook and the chaplain rush round to the front of the cart, the two last with glasses in their hands. The ordnance officer and a soldier come running to the cannon and try to push it along.

MOTHER COURAGE: What's the matter? Let me get my washing off the gun, you louts! *She tries to do so.*

THE OFFICER: The Catholics! Surprise attack! We don't know if we can get away! *To the soldier*: Get the gun! *He runs off.*

THE COOK: For heaven's sake! I must go to the Commander. Mother Courage, I'll be back in a day or two – for a short conversation. *He rushes off.*

MOTHER COURAGE: Hey, you've left your pipe!

THE COOK, *off*: Keep it for me, I'll need it!

MOTHER COURAGE: This *would* happen when we were just making money.

THE CHAPLAIN: Well, I must be going too. Yes, if the enemy's so close, it can be dangerous. 'Blessed are the peacemakers', a good slogan in wartime! If only I had a cloak.

MOTHER COURAGE: I'm lending no cloaks. Not even to save a life, I'm not. I've had experience in that line.

THE CHAPLAIN: But I'm in special danger. Because of my religion!

26

MOTHER COURAGE *brings him a cloak*: It's against my better judgment. Now run!

THE CHAPLAIN: I thank you, you're very generous, but maybe I'd better stay and sit here. If I run, I might attract the enemy's attention, I might arouse suspicion.

MOTHER COURAGE, *to the soldier*: Let it alone, you dolt, who's going to pay you for this? It'll cost you your life, let me hold it for you.

THE SOLDIER, *running away*: You're my witness: I tried!

MOTHER COURAGE: I'll swear to it! *Seeing Kattrin with the hat*: What on earth are you up to – with a whore's hat! Take it off this minute! Are you mad? With the enemy coming? *She tears the hat off her head*. Do you want them to find you and make a whore of you? And she has the boots on too, straight from Babylon. I'll soon settle that. *She tries to get them off*. Oh God, Chaplain, help me with these boots, I'll be back straightaway. *She runs to the wagon*.

YVETTE, *entering and powdering her face*: What's that you say: the Catholics are coming? Where's my hat? Who's been trampling on it? I can't run round in that, what will they think of me? And I've no mirror either. *To the chaplain*: How do I look – too much powder?

THE CHAPLAIN: Just, er, right.

YVETTE: And where are my red boots? *She can't find them because Kattrin is hiding her feet under her skirt*. I left them here! Now I've got to go barefoot to my tent, it's a scandal! *Exit*.

Swiss Cheese comes running in carrying a cash box.

MOTHER COURAGE *enters with her hands covered with ashes. To Kattrin*: Ashes! *To Swiss Cheese*: What have you got there?

SWISS CHEESE: The regimental cash box.

MOTHER COURAGE: Throw it away! Your paymastering days are over!

SWISS CHEESE: It's a trust! *He goes to the back*.

MOTHER COURAGE, *to the chaplain*: Off with your pastor's coat, Chaplain, or they'll recognize you, cloak or no cloak. *She is rubbing ashes into Kattrin's face.* Keep still. A little dirt, and you're safe. A calamity! The sentries were drunk. Well one must hide one's light under a bushel, as they say. When a soldier sees a clean face, there's one more whore in the world. Specially a Catholic soldier. For weeks on end, no grub. Then, when they get some by way of plunder, they jump on top of the womenfolk. That should do. Let me look at you. Not bad. Looks like you've been rolling in muck. Don't tremble. Nothing can happen to you now. *To Swiss Cheese*: Where've you left the cash box?

SWISS CHEESE: I thought I'd just put it in the wagon.

MOTHER COURAGE, *horrified*: What! In my wagon? God punish you for a prize idiot! If I just look away for a moment! They'll hang all three of us!

SWISS CHEESE: Then I'll put it somewhere else. Or escape with it.

MOTHER COURAGE: You'll stay where you are. It's too late.

THE CHAPLAIN, *still changing his clothes*: For Heaven's sake: the flag!

MOTHER COURAGE, *taking down the flag*: God in Heaven! I don't notice it any more. I've had it twenty-five years.

The thunder of cannon grows.

Three days later. Morning. The cannon is gone. Mother Courage, Kattrin, the chaplain and Swiss Cheese sit anxiously eating.

SWISS CHEESE: This is the third day I've been sitting here doing nothing, and the sergeant, who's always been patient with me, may be slowly beginning to ask, 'Where on earth is Swiss Cheese with that cash box?'

MOTHER COURAGE: Be glad they're not on the scent.

THE CHAPLAIN: What about me? I can't hold a service here or I'll be in hot water. It is written, 'Out of the abundance of the heart, the tongue speaketh.' But woe is me if *my* tongue speaketh!

MOTHER COURAGE: That's how it is. Here you sit – one with his religion, the other with his cash box, I don't know which is more dangerous.

28

THE CHAPLAIN: We're in God's hands now!

MOTHER COURAGE: I hope we're not as desperate as *that*, but it *is* hard to sleep at night. 'Course it'd be easier if *you* weren't here, Swiss Cheese, all the same I've not done badly. I told them I was against the Anti-Christ, who's a Swede with horns on his head. I told them I noticed his left horn's a bit threadbare. When they cross-questioned me, I always asked where I could buy holy candles a bit cheaper. I know these things because Swiss Cheese's father was a Catholic and made jokes about it. They didn't quite believe me but they needed a canteen, so they turned a blind eye. Maybe it's all for the best. We're prisoners. But so are lice in fur.

THE CHAPLAIN: The milk is good. As far as quantity goes, we may have to reduce our Swedish appetites somewhat. We are defeated.

MOTHER COURAGE: Who's defeated? The defeats and victories of the chaps at the top aren't always defeats and victories for the chaps at the bottom. Not at all. There've been cases where a defeat is a victory for the chaps at the bottom, it's only their honour that's lost, nothing serious. In Livonia once, our Chief took such a knock from the enemy, in the confusion I got a fine grey mare out of the baggage train, it pulled my wagon seven months – till we won and an inventory was taken. But in general both defeat and victory are a costly business for us that haven't got much. The best thing is for politics to get stuck in the mud. *To Swiss Cheese*: Eat!

SWISS CHEESE: I don't like it. How will the sergeant pay his men?

MOTHER COURAGE: Soldiers in flight don't get paid.

SWISS CHEESE: Well, they could claim to be. No pay, no flight. They can refuse to budge.

MOTHER COURAGE: Swiss Cheese, your sense of duty worries me. I've brought you up to be honest because you're not very bright. But don't go too far! And now I'm going with the chaplain to buy a Catholic flag and some meat. There's no one can hunt out meat like him, sure as a sleepwalker. He can tell a good piece of meat from the way his mouth waters. A good thing they let me stay in the business. In business you ask what price, not what religion. And Protestant trousers keep you just as warm.

THE CHAPLAIN: As the mendicant monk said when there was talk of the Lutherans standing everything on its head in town and country: Beggars will *always* be needed. *Mother Courage disappears into the wagon.* She's worried about the cash box. Up to now they've ignored us – as if we were part of the wagon – but can it last?

SWISS CHEESE: I can get rid of it.

THE CHAPLAIN: That's almost *more* dangerous. Suppose you're seen. They have spies. Yesterday morning one jumped out of the very hole I was relieving myself in. I was so off guard I almost broke out in prayer – *that* would have given me away all right! I believe their favourite way of finding a Protestant is smelling his, um, excrement. The spy was a little brute with a bandage over one eye.

MOTHER COURAGE, *clambering out of the wagon with a basket*: I've found you out, you shameless hussy! *She holds up Yvette's red boots in triumph.* Yvette's red boots! She just swiped them – because you went and told her she was a captivating person. *She lays them in the basket.* Stealing Yvette's boots! But *she* disgraces herself for money, *you* do it for nothing – for pleasure! I told you, you must wait for the peace. No soldiers! Save your proud, peacock ways for peacetime!

THE CHAPLAIN: I don't find her proud.

MOTHER COURAGE: Prouder than she can afford to be. I like her when people say 'I never noticed the poor thing'. I like her when she's a stone in Dalarna, where there's nothing but stones. *To Swiss Cheese*: Leave the cash box where it is, do you hear? And pay attention to your sister, she needs it. Between the two of you, you'll be the death of me yet. I'd rather take care of a bag of fleas.

She leaves with the chaplain. Kattrin clears the dishes away.

SWISS CHEESE: Not many days more when you can sit in the sun in your shirtsleeves. *Kattrin points to a tree.* Yes, the leaves are yellow already. *With gestures, Kattrin asks if he wants a drink.* I'm not drinking, I'm thinking. *Pause.* She says she can't sleep. So I *should* take the cash box away. I've found a place for it. I'll keep it in the mole hole by the river till the time comes. I might get it tonight before sunrise and take it to the regiment. How far can they have fled in three days? The sergeant's eyes'll pop out of his head. 'You've disappointed me most pleasantly, Swiss Cheese,' he'll say, '*I* trust you with the cash box and *you* bring it back!' Yes, Kattrin, I *will* have a glass now!

When Kattrin reappears behind the wagon two men confront her. One of them is a sergeant. The other doffs his hat and flourishes it in a showy greeting. He has a bandage over one eye.

THE MAN WITH THE BANDAGE: Good morning, young lady. Have you seen a man from the Second Protestant Regiment?

Terrified, Kattrin runs away, spilling her brandy. The two men look at each other and then withdraw after seeing Swiss Cheese.

SWISS CHEESE, *starting up from his reflection*: You're spilling it! What's the matter with you, can't you see where you're going? I don't understand you. Anyway, I must be off, I've decided it's the thing to do. *He stands up. She does all she can to make him aware of the danger he is in. He only pushes her away.* I'd like to know what you mean. I know you mean well, poor thing, you just can't get it out. And don't trouble yourself about the brandy, I'll live to drink so much of it, what's one glass? *He takes the cash box out of the wagon and puts it under his coat.* I'll be back straightaway. But don't hold me up or I'll have to scold you. Yes, I know you mean well. If you could only speak!

When she tries to hold him back he kisses her and pulls himself free. Exit. She is desperate and runs up and down, emitting little sounds. Mother Courage and the chaplain return. Kattrin rushes at her mother.

MOTHER COURAGE: What *is* it, what *is* it, Kattrin? Control yourself! Has someone done something to you? Where is Swiss

Cheese? *To the chaplain*: Don't stand around, get that Catholic flag up! *She takes a Catholic flag out of her basket and the chaplain runs it up the pole.*

THE CHAPLAIN, *bitterly*: All good Catholics forever!

MOTHER COURAGE: Now, Kattrin, calm down and tell all about it, your mother understands. What, that little bastard of mine's taken the cash box away! I'll box his ears for him, the rascal! Now take your time and don't try to talk, use your hands. I don't like it when you howl like a dog, what'll the chaplain think of you? You're giving him the creeps. A man with one eye was here?

THE CHAPLAIN: That fellow with one eye is an informer! Have they caught Swiss Cheese? *Kattrin shakes her head, shrugs her shoulders.* This is the end.

Voices off. The two men bring in Swiss Cheese.

SWISS CHEESE: Let me go. I've nothing on me. You're breaking my shoulder blade! I am innocent.

THE SERGEANT: This is where he comes from. These are his friends.

MOTHER COURAGE: Us? Since when?

SWISS CHEESE: I don't even know 'em. I was just getting my lunch here. Ten hellers it cost me. Maybe you saw me sitting on that bench. It was too salty.

THE SERGEANT: Who *are* you people, anyway?

MOTHER COURAGE: Law-abiding citizens! It's true what he says. He bought his lunch here. And it was too salty.

THE SERGEANT: Are you pretending you don't know him?

MOTHER COURAGE: I can't know all of them, can I? *I* don't ask, 'What's your name and are you a heathen?' If they pay up, they're not heathens to me. Are you a heathen?

SWISS CHEESE: Oh, no!

THE CHAPLAIN: He sat there like a law-abiding chap and never once opened his mouth. Except to eat. Which is necessary.

THE SERGEANT: Who do you think *you* are?

MOTHER COURAGE: Oh, he's my barman. And you're thirsty,

I'll bring you a glass of brandy. You must be footsore and weary!

THE SERGEANT: No brandy on duty. *To Swiss Cheese*: You were carrying something. You must have hidden it by the river. We saw the bulge in your shirt.

MOTHER COURAGE: Sure it was him?

SWISS CHEESE: I think you mean another fellow. There *was* a fellow with something under his shirt, I saw him. I'm the wrong man.

MOTHER COURAGE: I think so too. It's a misunderstanding. Could happen to anyone. Oh, I know what people are like, I'm Mother Courage, you've heard of me, everyone knows about me, and I can tell you this: he looks honest.

THE SERGEANT: We're after the regimental cash box. And we know what the man looks like who's been keeping it. We've been looking for him two days. It's you.

SWISS CHEESE: No, it's not!

THE SERGEANT: And if you don't shell out, you're dead, see? Where is it?

MOTHER COURAGE, *urgently*: 'Course he'd give it to you to save his life. He'd up and say, *I've* got it, here it is, you're stronger than me. He's not *that* stupid. Speak, little stupid, the sergeant's giving you a chance!

SWISS CHEESE: What if I *haven't* got it?

THE SERGEANT: Come with us. We'll get it out of you. *They take him off.*

MOTHER COURAGE, *shouting after them*: He'd tell you! He's not *that* stupid! And don't you break his shoulder blade! *She runs after them.*

The same evening. The Chaplain and Kattrin are rinsing glasses and polishing knives.

THE CHAPLAIN: Cases of people getting caught like this are by no means unknown in the history of religion. I am reminded of the Passion of Our Lord and Saviour. There's an old song about it. *He sings The Song of the Hours:*

33

In the first hour of the day
Simple Jesus Christ was
Presented as a murderer
To the heathen Pilate.

Pilate found no fault in him
No cause to condemn him
So he sent the Lord away.
Let King Herod see him!

Hour the third: the Son of God
Was with scourges beaten
And they set a crown of thorns
On the head of Jesus.

And they dressed him as a king
Joked and jested at him
And the cross to die upon
He himself must carry.

Six: they stripped Lord Jesus bare.
To the cross they nailed him.
When the blood came gushing, he
Prayed and loud lamented.

Each upon his cross, two thieves
Mocked him like the others.
And the bright sun crept away
Not to see such doings.

Nine: Lord Jesus cried aloud
That he was forsaken!
In a sponge upon a pole
Vinegar was fed him.

Then the Lord gave up the ghost
And the earth did tremble.
Temple curtain split in twain.
Rocks fell in the ocean.

34

Evening: they broke the bones
Of the malefactors.
Then they took a spear and pierced
The side of gentle Jesus.

And the blood and water ran
And they laughed at Jesus.
Of this simple son of man
Such and more they tell us.

MOTHER COURAGE, *entering, excited*: It's life and death. But the sergeant will still listen to us. The only thing is, he mustn't know it's our Swiss Cheese, or they'll say we helped him. It's only a matter of money, but where can *we* get money? Wasn't Yvette here? I met her on the way over. She's picked up a colonel! Maybe he'll buy her a canteen business!

THE CHAPLAIN: You'd sell the wagon, everything?

MOTHER COURAGE: Where else would I get the money for the sergeant?

THE CHAPLAIN: What are you to live off?

MOTHER COURAGE: That's just it.

Enter Yvette with a hoary old colonel.

YVETTE, *embracing Mother Courage*: Dear Mistress Courage, we meet again. *Whispering*: He didn't say no. *Aloud*: This is my friend, my, um, business adviser. I happened to hear you might sell your wagon. Due to special circumstances, I'd like to think about it.

MOTHER COURAGE: I want to pawn it, not sell it. And nothing hasty. In war time you don't find another wagon like that so easy.

YVETTE, *disappointed*: Only pawn it? I thought you wanted to sell. I don't know if I'm interested. *To the colonel*: What do *you* think, my dear?

THE COLONEL: I quite agree with you, ducky.

MOTHER COURAGE: It's only for pawn.

YVETTE: I thought you *had* to have the money.

MOTHER COURAGE, *firmly*: I do have to have it. But I'd rather

35

wear my feet off looking for an offer than just sell. We live off the wagon. It's an opportunity for you, Yvette. Who knows when you'll have another such? Who knows when you'll find another . . . business adviser?

THE COLONEL: Take it, take it!

YVETTE: My friend thinks I should go ahead, but I'm not sure, if it's only for pawn. You think we should buy it outright, don't you?

THE COLONEL: I do, ducky, I do!

MOTHER COURAGE: Then you must go and find something that's for sale. Maybe you'll find it – if you have the time, and your friend goes with you, let's say in about a week, or two weeks, you may find the right thing.

YVETTE: Yes, we can certainly look round for something. I love going around looking, I love going around with you, Poldy . . .

THE COLONEL: Really? Do you?

YVETTE: Oh, it's lovely! I could take two weeks of it!

THE COLONEL: Really, could you?

YVETTE: If you get the money, when are you thinking of paying it back?

MOTHER COURAGE: In two weeks. Maybe one.

YVETTE: I can't make up my mind. Poldy, advise me, *chéri*! *She takes the colonel to one side.* She'll *have* to sell, don't worry. That lieutenant – the blond one, you know the one I mean – he'll lend me the money. He's *mad* about me, he says I remind him of someone. What do you advise?

THE COLONEL: Oh, I have to warn you against *him*. He's no good. He'll exploit the situation. I told you, ducky, I told you *I'd* buy you something, didn't I tell you that?

YVETTE: I simply can't let you!

THE COLONEL: Oh, please, please!

YVETTE: Well, if you think the lieutenant might exploit the situation I *will* let you!

THE COLONEL: I do think so.

YVETTE: So you advise me to?

THE COLONEL: I do, ducky, I do!

YVETTE, *returning to Mother Courage*: My friend says all right.

36

Write me out a receipt saying the wagon's mine when the two weeks are up – with everything in it. I'll just run through it all now, the two hundred gilders can wait. *To the colonel*: You go ahead to the camp, I'll follow, I must go over all this so nothing'll be missing later from *my* wagon!

THE COLONEL: Wait, I'll help you up! *He does so.* Come soon, ducky-wucky! *Exit.*

MOTHER COURAGE: Yvette, Yvette!

YVETTE: There aren't many boots left!

MOTHER COURAGE: Yvette, this is no time to go through the wagon, yours or not yours. You promised you'd talk to the sergeant about Swiss Cheese. There isn't a minute to lose. He's up before the court martial one hour from now.

YVETTE: I just want to count these shirts again.

MOTHER COURAGE, *dragging her down the steps by the skirt*: You hyena, Swiss Cheese's life's at stake! And don't say who the money comes from. Pretend he's your sweetheart, for heaven's sake, or we'll all get it for helping him.

YVETTE: I've arranged to meet One Eye in the bushes. He must be there by now.

THE CHAPLAIN: And don't hand over all two hundred, a hundred and fifty's sure to be enough.

MOTHER COURAGE: Is it your money? I'll thank you to keep your nose out of this, I'm not doing *you* out of your porridge. Now run, and no haggling, remember his life's at stake. *She pushes Yvette off.*

THE CHAPLAIN: I didn't want to talk you into anything, but what are we going to live on? You have an unemployable daughter round your neck.

MOTHER COURAGE: I'm counting on that cash box, smart alec. They'll pay his expenses out of it.

THE CHAPLAIN: You think she can work it?

MOTHER COURAGE: It's in her own interest: I pay the two hundred and she gets the wagon. She knows what she's doing, she won't have her colonel on the string forever. Kattrin, go and clean the knives, use pumice stone. And don't *you* stand around like Jesus in Gethsemane. Get a move on, wash those

37

glasses. There'll be over fifty cavalrymen here tonight, and you'll be saying you're not used to being on your feet. 'Oh my poor feet, in church I never had to run round like this!' I think they'll let us have him. Thanks be to God they're corruptible. They're not wolves, they're human and after money. God is merciful, and men are bribable, that's how His will is done on earth as it is in Heaven. Corruption is our only hope. As long as there's corruption, there'll be merciful judges and even the innocent may get off.

YVETTE *comes panting in*: They'll do it for two hundred if you make it snappy – these things change from one minute to the next. I'd better take One Eye to my colonel at once. He confessed he had the cash box, they put the thumb-screws on him. But he threw it in the river when he noticed them coming up behind him. So it's gone. Shall I run and get the money from my colonel?

MOTHER COURAGE: The cash box gone? How'll I ever get my two hundred back?

YVETTE: So you thought you could get it from the cash box? I *would* have been sunk. Not a hope, Mother Courage. If you want your Swiss Cheese, you'll have to pay. Or should I let the whole thing drop, so you can keep your wagon?

MOTHER COURAGE: I wasn't reckoning on this. But you needn't hound me, you'll get the wagon, it's yours already, and it's been mine seventeen years. I need a minute to think it over, it's all so sudden. What can I do? I *can't* pay two hundred. I *should* have haggled with them. I must hold on to something, or any passer-by can kick me in the ditch. Go and say I'll pay a hundred and twenty or the deal's off. Even then I lose the wagon.

YVETTE: They won't do it. And anyway, One Eye's in a hurry. He keeps looking over his shoulder all the time, he's so worked up. Hadn't I better give them the whole two hundred?

MOTHER COURAGE, *desperate*: I can't pay it! I've been working thirty years. She's twenty-five and still no husband. I have her to think of. So leave me alone. I know what I'm doing. A hundred and twenty or no deal.

YVETTE: You know best. *She runs off.*

Mother Courage turns away and slowly walks a few paces to the rear. Then she turns round, looks neither at the chaplain nor her daughter, and sits down to help Kattrin polish the knives.

MOTHER COURAGE: Don't break the glasses, they're not ours. Watch what you're doing, you're cutting yourself. Swiss Cheese will be back, I'll give two hundred, if it's necessary. You'll get your brother back. With eighty gilders we could pack a hamper with goods and begin again. It wouldn't be the end of the world.

THE CHAPLAIN: The Bible says: the Lord will provide.

MOTHER COURAGE: You should rub them dry, I said.

They clean the knives in silence. Suddenly Kattrin runs sobbing behind the wagon.

YVETTE *comes running in*: They won't do it. I warned you. One Eye was going to drop it then and there. There's no point, he said. He said the drums would roll any second now and that's the sign a verdict has been pronounced. I offered a hundred and fifty, he didn't even shrug his shoulders. I could hardly get him to stay there while I came to you.

MOTHER COURAGE: Tell him, I'll pay two hundred. Run! *Yvette runs. Mother Courage sits, silent. The chaplain has stopped doing the glasses.* I believe – I've haggled too long.

In the distance, a roll of drums. The chaplain stands up and walks towards the rear. Mother Courage remains seated. It grows dark. It gets light again. Mother Courage has not moved.

YVETTE *appears, pale*: Now you've done it – with your haggling. You can keep the wagon now. He got eleven bullets, that's what. I don't know why I still bother about you, you don't deserve it, but I just happened to learn they don't think the cash box is really in the river. They suspect it's here, they think you have something to do with him. I think they're going to bring him here to see if you'll give yourself away when you see him. You'd better not know him or we're in for it. And I'd better tell you straight, they're just behind me.

Shall I keep Kattrin away? *Mother Courage shakes her head.* Does she know? Maybe she never heard the drums or didn't understand.

MOTHER COURAGE: She knows. Bring her.

Yvette brings Kattrin, who walks over to her mother and stands by her. Mother Courage takes her hand. Two men come on with a stretcher; there is a sheet on it and something underneath. Beside them, the sergeant. They put the stretcher down.

THE SERGEANT: Here's a man we don't know the name of. But he has to be registered to keep the records straight. He bought a meal from you. Look at him, see if you know him. *He pulls back the sheet.* Do you know him? *Mother Courage shakes her head.* What? You never saw him before he took that meal? *Mother Courage shakes her head.* Lift him up. Throw him in the carrion pit. He has no one that knows him.

They carry him off.

4

MOTHER COURAGE SINGS THE SONG OF THE GREAT
CAPITULATION

Outside an Officer's Tent

Mother Courage waits. A scrivener looks out of the tent.

THE SCRIVENER: I know you. You had a Protestant paymaster with you, he was hiding with you. Better make no complaint.

MOTHER COURAGE: I will too! I'm innocent and if I give up it'll look as if I have a bad conscience. They cut everything in my wagon to ribbons with their sabres and then claimed a fine of five thalers for nothing and less than nothing.

THE SCRIVENER: For your own good, keep your trap shut. We haven't many canteens, so we let you stay in business, especially if you've a bad conscience and have to pay a fine now and then.

MOTHER COURAGE: I'm going to file a complaint.

THE SCRIVENER: As you wish. Wait here till the captain has time. *He withdraws into the tent.*

A YOUNG SOLDIER *comes storming in*: Bugger the captain! Where *is* the son-of-a-bitch? Swiping my reward, spending it on brandy for his whores, I'll rip his belly open!

AN OLDER SOLDIER, *coming after him*: Shut your hole, you'll wind up in the stocks.

THE YOUNG SOLDIER: Come out, you thief, I'll make lamb chops out of you! I was the only one in the squad who swam the river and *he* grabs my money, I can't even buy myself a beer. Come on out! And let me slice you up!

THE OLDER SOLDIER: Holy Christ, he'll destroy himself!

THE YOUNG SOLDIER: Let me go or I'll run *you* down too. This has got to be settled!

THE OLDER SOLDIER: Saved the colonel's horse and didn't get the reward. He's young, he hasn't been at it long.

MOTHER COURAGE: Let him go. He doesn't have to be chained, he's not a dog. Very reasonable to want a reward. Why else should he want to shine?

THE YOUNG SOLDIER: He's in there pouring it down! You're all chickens. I've done something special, I want the reward!

MOTHER COURAGE: Young man, don't scream at *me*, I have my own troubles. And go easy with your voice, you may need it when the captain comes. The captain'll come and you'll be hoarse and can't make a sound, so he'll have to deny himself the pleasure of sticking you in the stocks till you pass out. The screamers don't scream long, only half an hour, after which they have to be sung to sleep, they're all in.

THE YOUNG SOLDIER: I'm not all in, and sleep's out of the question. I'm hungry. They're making their bread out of acorns and hemp-seed, and not even much of that. He's whoring on my money, and I'm hungry. I'll murder him!

MOTHER COURAGE: I understand: you're hungry. Last year your Commander ordered you people out of the streets and into the fields. So the crops got trampled down. I could have got ten gilders for boots, if anyone'd had ten gilders, and if I'd had any boots. He didn't expect to be around this year, but he is, and there's famine. I understand: you're angry.

THE YOUNG SOLDIER: It's no use your talking. I won't stand for injustice!

MOTHER COURAGE: You're quite right. But how long? How long won't you stand for injustice? One hour? Or two? You haven't asked yourself that, have you? And yet it's the main thing. It's pure misery to sit in the stocks. Especially if you leave it till then to decide you do stand for injustice.

THE YOUNG SOLDIER: I don't know why I listen to you. Bugger that captain! Where is he?

MOTHER COURAGE: You listen because you know I'm right. Your rage has calmed down already. It was a short one and you'd need a long one. But where would you find it?

THE YOUNG SOLDIER: Are you trying to say it's not right to ask for the money?

MOTHER COURAGE: Just the opposite. I only say, your rage won't last. You'll get nowhere with it, it's a pity. If your rage was a long one, I'd urge you on. Slice him up, I'd advise you. But what's the use if you *don't* slice him up because you can feel your tail between your legs? You stand there and the captain lets you have it.

THE OLDER SOLDIER: You're quite right, he's mad.

THE YOUNG SOLDIER: All right, we'll see whether I slice him up or not. *He draws his sword.* When he comes out, I slice him up!

THE SCRIVENER, *looking out*: The captain will be out in a minute. *In the tone of military command*: Be seated!

The young soldier sits.

MOTHER COURAGE: And he *is* seated. What did I tell you? You are seated. They know us through and through. They know how they must work it. Be seated! And we sit. And in sitting there's no revolt. Better not stand up again – not the way you did before – don't stand up again. And don't be embarrassed in front of me, I'm no better, not a scrap. We don't stick our necks out, do we, and why not? It wouldn't be good for

42

business. Let me tell you about the great capitulation. *She sings The Song of the Great Capitulation:*

Foldback

> Long, long ago, a green beginner
> I thought myself a special case.

(None of your ordinary run of the mill girls, with my looks and my talent and my love of the higher things!)

> I picked a hair out of my dinner
> And put the waiter in his place.

(All or nothing. Anyway, never the second best. I am the master of my fate. I'll take no orders from no one.)

> Then a little bird whispers!
> The bird says: 'Wait a year or so
> And marching with the band you'll go
> Keeping in step, now fast, now slow
> And piping out your little spiel.
> Then one day the battalions wheel
> And you go down upon your knees
> To God Almighty if you please!'

> My friend, before that year was over
> I'd learned to drink their cup of tea.

(Two children round your neck and the price of bread and what all!)

> When they were through with me, moreover
> They had me where they wanted me.

(You must get well in with people. If you scratch my back, I'll scratch yours. Never stick your neck out!)

> Then a little bird whispered!
> The bird says: 'Scarce a year or so
> And marching with the band she'd go
> Keeping in step, now fast, now slow

43

And piping out her little spiel.
Then one day the battalions wheel
And she goes down upon her knees
To God Almighty if you please!'

Our plans are big, our hopes colossal.
We hitch our wagon to a star.

(Where there's a will, there's a way. You can't hold a good man down.)

'We can lift mountains,' says the apostle.
And yet: how heavy one cigar!

(You must cut your coat according to your cloth.)

That little bird whispers!
The bird says: 'Wait a year or so
And marching with the band we go
Keeping in step, now fast, now slow
And piping out our little spiel.
Then one day the battalions wheel
And we go down upon our knees
To God Almighty if you please!'

And so I think you should stay here with your sword drawn if you're set on it and your anger is big enough. You have good cause, I admit. But if your anger is a short one, you'd better go.

THE YOUNG SOLDIER: Oh, shove it up! *He stumbles off, the other soldier following him.*

THE SCRIVENER *sticks his head out*: The captain is here. You can file your complaint.

MOTHER COURAGE: I've thought better of it. I'm not complaining. *Exit. The scrivener looks after her, shaking his head.*

5

TWO YEARS HAVE PASSED. THE WAR COVERS WIDER AND WIDER
TERRITORY. FOREVER ON THE MOVE, THE LITTLE WAGON
CROSSES POLAND, MORAVIA, BAVARIA, ITALY, AND AGAIN
BAVARIA. 1631. TILLY'S VICTORY AT MAGDEBURG, COSTS
MOTHER COURAGE FOUR OFFICERS' SHIRTS

The Wagon stands in a War-ruined Village

*Faint military music from the distance. Two soldiers are being served
at a counter by Kattrin and Mother Courage. One of them has a
woman's fur coat about his shoulders.*

MOTHER COURAGE: What, you can't pay? No money, no brandy!
They can play victory marches, they should pay their men.

THE FIRST SOLDIER: I want my brandy! I arrived too late for
plunder. The Chief allowed one hour to plunder the town,
it's a swindle. He's not inhuman, he says. So I suppose they
bought him off.

THE CHAPLAIN, *staggering in*: There are more in the farmhouse.
A family of peasants. Help me someone. I need linen!

*The second soldier goes with him. Kattrin is getting very excited.
She tries to get her mother to bring linen out.*

MOTHER COURAGE: I have none. I sold all my bandages to the
regiment. I'm not tearing up my officers' shirts for these
people.

THE CHAPLAIN, *calling over his shoulder*: I said I need linen!

MOTHER COURAGE, *stopping Kattrin from entering the wagon*: Not
a thing! They have nothing and they pay nothing!

THE CHAPLAIN, *to a woman he is carrying in*: Why did you stay
out there in the line of fire?

THE WOMAN: Our farm –

MOTHER COURAGE: Think they'd ever let go of *anything*? And
now I'm supposed to pay. Well, I won't!

THE FIRST SOLDIER: They're Protestants, why should they be
Protestants?

MOTHER COURAGE: Protestant, Catholic, what do *they* care? Their farm's gone, that's what.

THE SECOND SOLDIER: They're not Protestants anyway, they're Catholics.

THE FIRST SOLDIER: In a bombardment we can't pick and choose.

A PEASANT, *brought on by the chaplain*: My arm's gone.

THE CHAPLAIN: Where's that linen?

All look at Mother Courage, who does not budge.

MOTHER COURAGE: I can't give you any. With all I have to pay out – taxes, duties, bribes . . . *Kattrin takes up a board and threatens her mother with it, emitting gurgling sounds.* Are you out of your mind? Put that board down or I'll fetch you one, you lunatic! I'm giving nothing, I daren't, I have myself to think of. *The chaplain lifts her bodily off the steps of the wagon and sets her down on the ground. He takes out shirts from the wagon and tears them in strips.* My shirts, my officers' shirts! *From the house comes the cry of a child in pain.*

THE PEASANT: The child's still in there! *Kattrin runs in.*

THE CHAPLAIN, *to the woman*: Stay where you are. She's getting it for you.

MOTHER COURAGE: Hold her back, the roof may fall in!

THE CHAPLAIN: I'm not going back in there!

MOTHER COURAGE, *pulled in both directions*: Go easy on my expensive linen.

The second soldier holds her back. Kattrin brings a baby out of the ruins.

MOTHER COURAGE: Another baby to drag around, you must be pleased with yourself. Give it to its mother this minute! Or do I have to fight you again for hours till I get it from you? Are you deaf? *To the second soldier*: Don't stand about gawking, go back there and tell 'em to stop that music, I can see their victory without it. I have nothing but losses from your victory!

THE CHAPLAIN, *bandaging*: The blood's coming through.

Kattrin is rocking the child and half humming a lullaby.

46

MOTHER COURAGE: There she sits, happy as a lark in all this misery. Give the baby back, the mother is coming to! *She sees the first soldier. He had been handling the drinks, and is now trying to make off with the bottle.* God's truth! You beast! You want another victory, do you? Then pay for it!

THE FIRST SOLDIER: I have nothing.

MOTHER COURAGE, *snatching the fur coat back*: Then leave this coat, it's stolen goods anyhow.

THE CHAPLAIN: There's still someone in there.

6

BEFORE THE CITY OF INGOLSTADT IN BAVARIA MOTHER COURAGE IS PRESENT AT THE FUNERAL OF THE FALLEN COMMANDER TILLY. CONVERSATIONS TAKE PLACE ABOUT WAR HEROES AND THE DURATION OF THE WAR. THE CHAPLAIN COMPLAINS THAT HIS TALENTS ARE LYING FALLOW AND KATTRIN GETS THE RED BOOTS. THE YEAR IS 1632

The inside of a Canteen Tent Q3B Rain.

The inner side of a counter at the rear. Rain. In the distance, drums and funeral music. The chaplain and the regimental scrivener are playing draughts. Mother Courage and her daughter are taking an inventory.

THE CHAPLAIN: The funeral procession is just starting out.

MOTHER COURAGE: Pity about the Chief – twenty-two pairs of socks – getting killed that way. They say it was an accident. There was a fog over the fields that morning, and the fog was to blame. The Chief called up another regiment, told 'em to fight to the death, rode back again, missed his way in the fog, went forward instead of back, and ran smack into a bullet in the thick of the battle – only four lanterns left. *A whistle from the rear. She goes to the counter. To a soldier*: It's a disgrace the way you're all skipping your Commander's funeral! *She pours a drink.*

THE SCRIVENER: They shouldn't have handed the money out

before the funeral. Now the men are all getting drunk instead of going to it.

THE CHAPLAIN, *to the scrivener*: Don't you have to be there?

THE SCRIVENER: I stayed away because of the rain.

MOTHER COURAGE: It's different for you, the rain might spoil your uniform. I hear they wanted to ring the bells for his funeral, which is natural, but it came out that the churches had been shot up by his orders, so the poor Commander won't be hearing any bells when they lower him in his grave. Instead, they'll fire off three shots so the occasion won't be *too* sober – sixteen leather belts.

A VOICE FROM THE COUNTER: Service! One brandy!

MOTHER COURAGE: Your money first. No, you *can't* come inside the tent, not with those boots on. You can drink outside, rain or no rain. I only let officers in here. *To the scrivener*: The Chief had his troubles lately, I hear. There was unrest in the Second Regiment because he didn't pay 'em but he said it was a war of religion and they must fight it free of charge.

Funeral March. All look towards the rear.

THE CHAPLAIN: Now they're filing past the body.

MOTHER COURAGE: I feel sorry for a commander or an emperor like that – when he might have had something special in mind, something they'd talk about in times to come, something they'd raise a statue to him for. The conquest of the world now, *that's* a goal for a commander, he wouldn't know any better. . . . Lord, worms have got into the biscuits. . . . In short, he works his hands to the bone and then it's all spoiled by the common riffraff that only wants a jug of beer or a bit of company, not the higher things in life. The finest plans have always been spoiled by the littleness of them that should carry them out. Even emperors can't do it all by themselves. They count on support from their soldiers and the people round about. Am I right?

THE CHAPLAIN, *laughing*: You're right, Mother Courage, till you come to the soldiers. They do what they can. Those chaps outside, for example, drinking their brandy in the rain, I'd trust 'em to fight a hundred years, one war after another, **two** at a time if necessary. And I wasn't trained as a commander.

MOTHER COURAGE: . . . Seventeen leather belts. . . . Then you don't think the war might end?

THE CHAPLAIN: Because a commander's dead? Don't be childish, they're sixpence a dozen. There are always heroes.

MOTHER COURAGE: Well, I wasn't asking for the sake of argument. I was wondering if I should buy up a lot of supplies. They happen to be cheap just now. But if the war ended, I might just as well throw them away.

THE CHAPLAIN: I realize you are serious, Mother Courage. Well, there've always been people going round saying some day the war will end. I say, you can't be sure the war will *ever* end. Of course it may have to pause occasionally – for breath, as it were – it can even meet with an accident – nothing on this earth is perfect – a war of which we could say if left nothing to be desired will probably never exist. A war can come to a sudden halt – from unforeseen causes – you can't think of everything – a little oversight, and the war's in the hole, and someone's got to pull it out again! The someone is the Emperor or the King or the Pope. They're such friends in need, the war has really nothing to worry about, it can look forward to a prosperous future.

A SOLDIER *sings at the counter*:

> One schnapps, mine host, be quick, make haste!
> A soldier's got no time to waste:
> He must be shooting, shooting, shooting
> His Kaiser's enemies uprooting!

Make it a double. This is a holiday.

MOTHER COURAGE: If I was sure you're right . . .

THE CHAPLAIN: Think it out for yourself: how *could* the war end?

THE SOLDIER, *off stage*:

> Two breasts, my girl, be quick, make haste!
> A soldier's got no time to waste:
> He must be hating, hating, hating
> He cannot keep his Kaiser waiting!

49

THE SCRIVENER, *suddenly* What about peace? Yes, peace. I'm from Bohemia. I'd like to get home once in a while.

THE CHAPLAIN: Oh, you would, would you? Dear old peace! What happens to the hole when the cheese is gone?

THE SOLDIER, *off stage*:

Your blessing, priest, be quick, make haste!

A soldier's got no time to waste:

He must be dying, dying, dying

His Kaiser's greatness glorifying!

THE SCRIVENER: In the long run you can't live without peace!

THE CHAPLAIN: Well, I'd say there's peace even in war, war has its islands of peace. For war satisfies *all* needs, even those of peace, yes, they're provided for, or the war couldn't keep going. In war – as in the very thick of peace – you can take a crap, and between one battle and the next there's always a beer, and even on the march you can snatch a nap – on your elbow maybe, in a gutter – something can always be managed. Of course you can't play cards during an attack, but neither can you while ploughing the fields in peace time; it's when the victory's won that there are possibilities. You have your leg shot off, and at first you raise quite an outcry as if it *was* something, but soon you calm down or take a swig of brandy, and you end up hopping about, and the war is none the worse for your little misadventure. And can't you be fruitful and multiply in the thick of slaughter – behind a barn or somewhere? Nothing can keep you from it very long in any event. And so the war has your offspring and can carry on. War is like love, it always finds a way. Why *should* it end?

Kattrin has stopped working. She stares at the chaplain.

MOTHER COURAGE: Then I *will* buy those supplies, I'll rely on you. *Kattrin suddenly bangs a basket of glasses down on the ground and runs out. Mother Courage laughs.* Kattrin! Lord, Kattrin's still going to wait for peace. I promised her she'll get a husband – when it's peace. *She runs after her.*

THE SCRIVENER, *standing up*: I win. You were talking. You pay.

MOTHER COURAGE, *returning with Kattrin*: Be sensible, the war'll go on a bit longer, and we'll make a bit more money, then peace'll be all the nicer. Now you go into the town, it's not ten minutes walk, and bring the things from the Golden Lion, just the dearer ones, we can get the rest later in the wagon. It's all arranged, the clerk will go with you, most of the soldiers are at the Commander's funeral, nothing can happen to you. Do a good job, don't lose anything, Kattrin, think of your trousseau!

Kattrin ties a cloth round her head and leaves with the scrivener.

THE CHAPLAIN: You don't mind her going with the scrivener?

MOTHER COURAGE: She's not so pretty anyone would want to ruin her.

THE CHAPLAIN: The way you run your business and always come through is highly commendable, Mother Courage – I see how you got your name.

MOTHER COURAGE: The poor need courage. They're lost, that's why. That they even get up in the morning is something – in *their* plight. Or that they plough a field – in war time. Even their bringing children into the world shows they have courage, for they have no prospects. They have to hang each other one by one and slaughter each other in the lump, so if they want to look each other in the face once in a while, well, it takes courage. That they put up with an Emperor and a Pope, that takes an unnatural amount of courage, for *they* cost you your life. *She sits, takes a small pipe from her pocket and smokes it.* You might chop me a bit of firewood.

THE CHAPLAIN, *reluctantly taking his coat off and preparing to chop wood*: Properly speaking, I'm a pastor of souls, not a woodcutter.

MOTHER COURAGE: But I don't have a soul. And I do need wood.

THE CHAPLAIN: What's that little pipe you've got there?

MOTHER COURAGE: Just a pipe.

THE CHAPLAIN: I think it's a very particular pipe.

MOTHER COURAGE: Oh?

THE CHAPLAIN: The cook's pipe in fact. The cook from the Oxenstierna Regiment.

MOTHER COURAGE: If you know, why beat about the bush?

THE CHAPLAIN: Because I don't know if you've been *aware* that's what you've been smoking. It was possible you just rummaged among your belongings and your fingers just lit on a pipe and you just took it. In pure absent-mindedness.

MOTHER COURAGE: How do you know that's not it?

THE CHAPLAIN: It isn't. You *are* aware of it. *He brings the axe down on the block with a crash.*

MOTHER COURAGE: What if I was?

THE CHAPLAIN: I must give you a warning, Mother Courage, it's my duty. You are unlikely ever again to see the gentleman but that's no pity, you're in luck. Mother Courage, he did not impress me as trustworthy. On the contrary.

MOTHER COURAGE: Really? He was such a nice man.

THE CHAPLAIN: Well! So that's what you call a nice man. I do not. *The axe falls again.* Far be it from me to wish him ill, but I cannot – cannot – describe him as nice. No, no, he's a Don Juan, a cunning Don Juan. Just look at that pipe if you don't believe me. You must admit it tells all.

MOTHER COURAGE: I see nothing special in it. It's been, um, used.

THE CHAPLAIN: It's bitten half-way through! He's a man of great violence! It is the pipe of a man of great violence, you can see *that* if you've any judgment left! *He deals the block a tremendous blow.*

MOTHER COURAGE: Don't bite my chopping block half-way through!

THE CHAPLAIN: I told you I had no training as a woodcutter. The care of souls was my field. Around here my gifts and capabilities are grossly misused. In physical labour my god-given talents find no – um – adequate expression – which is a sin. You haven't heard me preach. Why, I can put such spirit into a regiment with a single sermon that the enemy's a mere flock of sheep to them and their own lives no more than smelly old shoes to be thrown away at the thought of final victory! God has given me the gift of tongues. I can preach you out of your senses!

MOTHER COURAGE: I need my senses. What would I do without them?

THE CHAPLAIN: Mother Courage, I have often thought that – under a veil of plain speech – you conceal a heart. You are human, you need warmth.

MOTHER COURAGE: The best way of warming this tent is to chop plenty of firewood.

THE CHAPLAIN: You're changing the subject. Seriously, my dear Courage, I sometimes ask myself how it would be if our relationship should be somewhat more firmly cemented. I mean, now the wind of war has whirled us so strangely together.

MOTHER COURAGE: The cement's pretty firm already. I cook your meals. And you lend a hand – at chopping firewood, for instance.

THE CHAPLAIN, *going over to her, gesturing with the axe*: You know what I mean by a close relationship. It has nothing to do with eating and woodcutting and such base necessities. Let your heart speak!

MOTHER COURAGE: Don't come at me like that with your axe, that'd be *too* close a relationship!

THE CHAPLAIN: This is no laughing matter, I am in earnest. I've thought it all over.

MOTHER COURAGE: Dear Chaplain, be a sensible fellow. I like you, and I don't want to heap coals of fire on your head. All I'm after is to bring me and my children through in that wagon. It isn't just mine, the wagon, and anyway, I've no mind to start having a private life. At the moment I'm taking quite a risk buying these things when the Commander's fallen and there's all this talk of peace. Where would you go, if I was ruined? See? You don't even know. Now chop some firewood and it'll be warm of an evening, which is quite a lot in times like these. What was that? *She stands up. Kattrin enters, breathless, with a wound across the eye and forehead. She is dragging all sorts of articles, parcels, leather goods, a drum, etc.* What is it, were you attacked? On the way back? She was attacked on the way back! I'll bet it was that soldier who got drunk on my liquor. I should never have let you go. Dump all that stuff! It's not bad, the wound is only a flesh wound. I'll bandage it for you, it'll be all healed up in a week. They're worse than animals. *She bandages the wound.*

THE CHAPLAIN: I reproach them with nothing. At home they never did these shameful things. The men who start the wars are responsible, they bring out the worst in people.

MOTHER COURAGE: Didn't the scrivener walk you back home? That's because you're a respectable girl, he thought they'd leave you alone. The wound's not at all deep, it will never show. There: all bandaged up. Now, I've got something for you, rest easy. A secret. I've been holding it, you'll see. *She digs Yvette's red boots out of a bag.* Well, what do you see? You always wanted them. Now you have them. *She helps her to put the boots on.* Put them on quick, before I'm sorry I let you have them. It will never show, though it wouldn't bother *me* if it did. The fate of the ones they like is the worst. They drag them round with them till they're finished. A girl they don't care for they leave alone. I've seen so many girls, pretty as they come in the beginning, then all of a sudden they looked a fright – enough to scare a wolf. They can't even go behind a tree on the street without having something to fear from it. They lead a frightful life. Like with trees: the tall, straight ones are cut down for roof timber, and the crooked ones can enjoy life. So this wound here is really a piece of luck. The boots have kept well. I gave them a good clean before I put them away.

Kattrin leaves the boots and creeps into the wagon.

THE CHAPLAIN, *when she's gone*: I hope she won't be disfigured?

MOTHER COURAGE: There'll be a scar. She needn't wait for peace now.

THE CHAPLAIN: She didn't let them get any of the stuff away from her.

MOTHER COURAGE: Maybe I shouldn't have made such a point

of it. If only I ever knew what went on inside her head. Once she stayed out all night, once in all the years. I could never get out of her what happened. I racked my brains for quite a while. *She picks up the things Kattrin spilled and sorts them angrily.* This is war. A nice source of income, I must say!

Cannon shots. Q4 Cannon salute.

THE CHAPLAIN: Now they're lowering the Commander into his grave! A historic moment.

MOTHER COURAGE: It's a historic moment to me when they hit my daughter over the eye. She's all but finished now, she'll never get a husband, and she's so mad about children! Even her dumbness comes from the war. A soldier stuck something in her mouth when she was little. I'll not see Swiss Cheese again, and where my Eilif is the Good Lord knows. Curse the war!

7

MOTHER COURAGE AT THE HEIGHT OF HER BUSINESS CAREER

A Highway

The chaplain, Mother Courage, and her daughter Kattrin pull the wagon, and new wares are hanging from it. Mother Courage wears a necklace of silver coins.

MOTHER COURAGE: I won't let you spoil my war for me. Destroys the weak, does it? Well, what does peace do for 'em, huh? War feeds its people better. *She sings:* Foldback

> If war don't suit your disposition
> When victory comes you will be dead.
> War is a business proposition:
> Not with cream-cheese but steel and lead.

And staying in one place won't help either. Those who stay at home are the first to go. *She sings:*

Too many seek a bed to sleep in:
Each ditch is taken, and each cave
And he who digs a hole to creep in
Finds he has dug an early grave.
And many a man spends many a minute
In hurrying towards some resting place.
You wonder, when at last he's in it
Just why the fellow forced the pace.

The wagon proceeds.

8

1632. IN THIS SAME YEAR GUSTAVUS ADOLPHUS FELL IN THE BATTLE OF LÜTZEN. THE PEACE THREATENS MOTHER COURAGE WITH RUIN. HER BRAVE SON PERFORMS ONE HEROIC DEED TOO MANY AND COMES TO A SHAMEFUL END.

A Camp

A summer morning. In front of the wagon, an old woman and her son. The son is dragging a large bag of bedding.

MOTHER COURAGE, *from inside the wagon*: Must you come at the crack of dawn?

THE YOUNG MAN: We've been walking all night, twenty miles it was, we have to be back today.

MOTHER COURAGE, *still inside*: What do I want with bed feathers? People don't even have houses.

THE YOUNG MAN: At least wait till you see 'em.

THE OLD WOMAN: Nothing doing here either, let's go.

THE YOUNG MAN: And let 'em sign away the roof over our heads for taxes? Maybe she'll pay three gilders if you throw in that bracelet. *Bells start ringing.* You hear, mother?

VOICES *from the rear*: It's peace! The King of Sweden's been killed!

MOTHER COURAGE *sticks her head out of the wagon. She hasn't done her hair yet*: Bells! What are the bells for, middle of the week?

56

THE CHAPLAIN, *crawling out from under the wagon*: What's that they're shouting?

THE YOUNG MAN: It's peace.

THE CHAPLAIN: Peace!

MOTHER COURAGE: Don't tell me peace has broken out – when I've just done and bought all these supplies!

THE CHAPLAIN, *calling, towards the rear*: Is it peace?

VOICE, *from a distance*: They say the war stopped three weeks ago. I've only just heard.

THE CHAPLAIN, *to Mother Courage*: Or why would they ring the bells?

VOICE: A great crowd of Lutherans have just arrived with wagons – they brought the news.

THE YOUNG MAN: It's peace, mother. *The old woman collapses.* What's the matter?

MOTHER COURAGE, *back in the wagon*: Kattrin, it's peace! Put on your black dress, we're going to church, we owe it to Swiss Cheese! Can it be true?

THE YOUNG MAN: The people here say so too, the war's over. Can you stand up? *The old woman stands up, dazed.* I'll get the harness shop going again now, I promise you. Everything'll be all right, father will get his bed back. . . . Can you walk? *To the chaplain*: She felt ill, it was the news. She didn't believe there'd ever be peace again. Father always said there would. We're going home. *They leave.*

MOTHER COURAGE, *off*: Give her some brandy.

THE CHAPLAIN: They've left already.

MOTHER COURAGE, *still off*: What's going on in the camp over there?

THE CHAPLAIN: They're all getting together. I think I'll go over. Shall I put my pastor's coat on again?

MOTHER COURAGE: Better get the exact news first, and not risk being taken for the Antichrist. I'm glad about the peace even though I'm ruined. At least I've got two of my children through the war. Now I'll see my Eilif again.

THE CHAPLAIN: And who may this be coming down from the camp? Well, if it isn't our Swedish Commander's cook!

THE COOK, *somewhat bedraggled, carrying a bundle*: Who's here? The chaplain!

THE CHAPLAIN: Mother Courage, a visitor!

Mother Courage clambers out.

THE COOK: Well, I promised I'd come over for a brief conversation as soon as I had time. I didn't forget your brandy, Mrs. Fierling.

MOTHER COURAGE: Jesus, the Commander's cook! After all these years! Where is Eilif, my eldest?

THE COOK: Isn't he here yet? He went on ahead yesterday, he was on his way over.

THE CHAPLAIN: I *will* put my pastor's clothes on. I'll be back. *He goes behind the wagon.*

MOTHER COURAGE: He may be here any minute then. *She calls towards the wagon*: Kattrin, Eilif's coming! Bring a glass of brandy for the cook, Kattrin! *Kattrin doesn't come.* Pull your hair over it and have done. Mr. Lamb is no stranger. *She gets the brandy herself.* She won't come out. Peace is nothing to her, it was too long coming. They hit her right over the eye. You can hardly see it now. But she thinks people stare at her.

THE COOK: Ah yes, war! *He and Mother Courage sit.*

MOTHER COURAGE: Cook, you come at a bad time: I'm ruined.

THE COOK: What? That's terrible!

MOTHER COURAGE: The peace has broken my neck. On the chaplain's advice I've gone and bought a lot of supplies. Now everybody's leaving and I'm holding the baby.

THE COOK: How could you listen to the chaplain? If I'd had time – but the Catholics were too quick for me – I'd have warned you against him. He's a windbag. Well, so now he's the big man round here!

MOTHER COURAGE: He's been doing the dishes for me and helping with the wagon.

THE COOK: With the wagon – him! And I'll bet he's told you a few of his jokes. He has a most unhealthy attitude to women. I tried to influence him but it was no good. He isn't sound.

MOTHER COURAGE: Are you sound?

THE COOK: If I'm nothing else, I'm sound. Your health!

MOTHER COURAGE: Sound! Only one person around here was ever sound, and I never had to slave as I did then. He sold the blankets off the children's beds in the spring, and he found my mouth-organ unchristian. You aren't recommending yourself if you *admit* you're sound.

THE COOK: You fight tooth and nail, don't you? I like that.

MOTHER COURAGE: Don't tell me you've been dreaming of my teeth and nails.

THE COOK: Well, here we sit, while the bells of peace do ring, and you pouring your famous brandy as only you know how!

MOTHER COURAGE: I don't think much of the bells of peace at the moment. I don't see how they can hand out all this pay that's in arrears. And then where shall I be with my famous brandy? Have you all been paid?

THE COOK, *hesitating*: Not exactly. That's why we disbanded. In the circumstances, I thought, why stay? For the time being, I'll look up a couple of friends. So here I sit – with you.

MOTHER COURAGE: In other words, you're broke.

THE COOK, *annoyed by the bells*: It's about time they stopped that racket! I'd like to set myself up in some business. I'm fed up with being their cook. I'm supposed to make do with tree roots and shoe leather, and then they throw my hot soup in my face! Being a cook nowadays is a dog's life. I'd sooner do war service, but of course it's peace now. *As the chaplain turns up, wearing his old coat*: We'll talk it over later.

THE CHAPLAIN: The coat's pretty good. Just a few moth holes.

THE COOK: I don't know why you take the trouble. You won't find another job. Who could you incite now to earn an honest living or risk his life for a cause? Besides, I have a bone to pick with you.

THE CHAPLAIN: Have you?

THE COOK: I have. You advised a lady to buy superfluous goods on the pretext that the war would never end.

THE CHAPLAIN, *hotly*: I'd like to know what business it is of yours?

THE COOK: It's unprincipled behaviour! How can you give unwanted advice? And interfere with the conduct of other people's businesses?

THE CHAPLAIN: Who's interfering now, I'd like to know? *To Mother Courage*: I had no idea you were such a close friend of this gentleman and had to account to *him* for everything.

MOTHER COURAGE: Now don't get excited. The cook's giving his personal opinion. You can't deny your war was a frost.

THE CHAPLAIN: You mustn't take the name of peace in vain, Courage. Remember, you're a hyena of the battlefield!

MOTHER COURAGE: A what?

THE COOK: If you insult my girl friend, you'll have to reckon with me!

THE CHAPLAIN: I am *not* speaking to you, your intentions are only too transparent! *To Mother Courage*: But when I see *you* take peace between finger and thumb like a snotty old hanky, my humanity rebels! It shows that you want war, not peace, for what you get out of it. But don't forget the proverb: he who sups with the devil must use a long spoon!

MOTHER COURAGE: Remember what one fox said to another that was caught in a trap? 'If you stay there, you're just asking for trouble!' There isn't much love lost between me and the war. And when it comes to calling me a hyena, you and I part company.

THE CHAPLAIN: Then why all this grumbling about the peace just as everyone's heaving a sigh of relief? Is it for the junk in your wagon?

MOTHER COURAGE: My goods are not junk. I live off them. *You've* been living off them.

THE CHAPLAIN: You live off war. Exactly.

THE COOK, *to the chaplain*: As a grown man, who should know better than to go around advising people. *To Mother Courage*: Now, in your situation you'd be wise to get rid of certain goods at once – before the prices sink to nothing. Get ready and get going, there isn't a moment to lose!

MOTHER COURAGE: That's sensible advice, I think I'll take it.

THE CHAPLAIN: Because the cook says so.

MOTHER COURAGE: Why didn't *you* say so? He's right, I must get to the market. *She climbs into the wagon.*

THE COOK: One up for me, chaplain. You have no presence of mind. You should have said, '*I* gave you advice? Why, I was just talking politics!' And you shouldn't take me on as a rival. Cockfights are not becoming to your cloth.

THE CHAPLAIN: If you don't shut your trap, I'll murder you, cloth or no cloth!

THE COOK, *taking his boots off and unwinding the wrappings on his feet*: If you hadn't degenerated into a godless tramp, you could easily get yourself a parsonage, now it's peace. Cooks won't be needed, there's nothing to cook, but there's still plenty to believe, and people are prepared to go on believing it.

THE CHAPLAIN: Mr. Lamb, please don't drive me out! Since I became a tramp, I'm a somewhat better man. I couldn't preach to 'em any more.

Yvette Pottier enters, decked out in black, with a stick. She is much older, fatter, and heavily powdered. Behind her, a servant.

YVETTE: Hullo, everybody! Is this Mother Courage's establishment?

THE CHAPLAIN: Quite right. And with whom have we the pleasure?

YVETTE: I am Madame Colonel Starhemberg, good people. Where's Mother Courage?

THE CHAPLAIN, *calling to the wagon*: Madame Colonel Starhemberg wants to speak to you!

MOTHER COURAGE, *from inside*: Coming!

YVETTE, *calling*: It's Yvette!

MOTHER COURAGE, *inside*: Yvette!

YVETTE: Just to see how you're getting on! *As the cook turns round in horror*: Peter!

THE COOK: Yvette!

YVETTE: Of all things! How did *you* get here?

THE COOK: On a cart.

THE CHAPLAIN: Well! You know each other? Intimately?

YVETTE: Not half. *Scrutinizing the cook*: You're fat.

61

THE COOK: For that matter, *you're* no beanpole.

YVETTE: Anyway, nice meeting you, tramp. Now I can tell you what I think of you.

THE CHAPLAIN: Do so, tell him all, but wait till Mother Courage comes out.

THE COOK: Now don't make a scene . . .

MOTHER COURAGE *comes out, laden with goods*: Yvette! *They embrace.* But why are you in mourning?

YVETTE: Doesn't it suit me? My husband, the colonel, died several years ago.

MOTHER COURAGE: The old fellow that nearly bought my wagon?

YVETTE: His elder brother.

MOTHER COURAGE: So you're not doing badly. Good to see one person who got somewhere in the war.

YVETTE: I've had my ups and downs.

MOTHER COURAGE: Don't let's speak ill of colonels. They make money like hay.

THE CHAPLAIN, *to the cook*: If I were you, I'd put my shoes on again. *To Yvette*: You promised to give us your opinion of this gentleman.

THE COOK: Now, Yvette, don't make a stink!

MOTHER COURAGE: He's a friend of mine, Yvette.

YVETTE: He's – Peter Piper, that's who.

MOTHER COURAGE: What!

THE COOK: Cut the nicknames. My name's Lamb.

MOTHER COURAGE, *laughing*: Peter Piper? Who turned the women's heads? And I've been keeping your pipe for you.

THE CHAPLAIN: And smoking it.

YVETTE: Lucky I can warn you against him. He's a bad lot. You won't find a worse on the whole coast of Flanders. He got more girls in trouble than . . .

THE COOK: That's a long time ago, it isn't true any more.

YVETTE: Stand up when you talk to a lady! Oh, how I loved that man! And all the time he was having a little bowlegged brunette. He got *her* into trouble too, of course.

THE COOK: I seem to have brought *you* luck!

YVETTE: Shut your trap, you hoary ruin! And you take care,

Mother Courage, this type is still dangerous even in decay!

MOTHER COURAGE, *to Yvette*: Come with me, I must get rid of this stuff before the prices fall.

YVETTE, *concentrating on the cook*: Miserable cur!

MOTHER COURAGE: Maybe you can help me at army headquarters, you have contacts.

YVETTE: Damnable whore hunter!

MOTHER COURAGE, *shouting into the wagon*: Kattrin, church is all off, I'm going to market!

YVETTE: Inveterate seducer!

MOTHER COURAGE, *still to Kattrin*: When Eilif comes, give him something to drink!

YVETTE: That a man of *his* ilk should have been able to turn me from the straight and narrow! I have only my own star to thank that I rose nonetheless to the heights! But I've put an end to your tricks, Peter Piper, and one day – in a better life than this – the Lord God will reward me! Come, Mother Courage! *She leaves with Mother Courage.*

THE CHAPLAIN: As our text this morning let us take the saying, the mills of God grind slowly. And you complain of my jokes!

THE COOK: I never have any luck. I'll be frank, I was hoping for a good hot dinner, I'm starving. And now they'll be talking about me, and she'll get a completely wrong picture. I think I should go before she comes back.

THE CHAPLAIN: I think so too.

THE COOK: Chaplain, peace makes me sick. Mankind must perish by fire and sword, we're born and bred in sin! Oh, how I wish I was roasting a great fat capon for the Commander – God knows where *he's* got to – with mustard sauce and those little yellow carrots . . .

THE CHAPLAIN: Red cabbage – with capon, red cabbage.

THE COOK: You're right. But he always wanted yellow carrots.

THE CHAPLAIN: He never understood a thing.

THE COOK: You always put plenty away.

THE CHAPLAIN: Under protest.

THE COOK: Anyway, you must admit, those were the days.

THE CHAPLAIN: Yes, that I might admit.

THE COOK: Now you've called her a hyena, there's not much future for you here either. What are you staring at?

THE CHAPLAIN: It's Eilif! *Followed by two soldiers with halberds, Eilif enters. His hands are fettered. He is white as chalk.* What's happened to you?

EILIF: Where's mother?

THE CHAPLAIN: Gone to town.

EILIF: They said she was here. I was allowed a last visit.

THE COOK, *to the soldiers*: Where are you taking him?

A SOLDIER: For a ride.

The other soldier makes the gesture of throat cutting.

THE CHAPLAIN: What has he done?

THE SOLDIER: He broke in on a peasant. The wife is dead.

THE CHAPLAIN: Eilif, how could you?

EILIF: It's no different. It's what I did before.

THE COOK: That was in wartime.

EILIF: Shut your hole. Can I sit down till she comes?

THE SOLDIER: No.

THE CHAPLAIN: It's true. In war time they honoured him for it. He sat at the Commander's right hand. It was bravery. Couldn't we speak with the provost?

THE SOLDIER: What's the use? Stealing cattle from a peasant, what's brave about that?

THE COOK: It was just stupid.

EILIF: If I'd been stupid, I'd have starved, clever dick.

THE COOK: So you were bright and paid for it.

THE CHAPLAIN: At least we must bring Kattrin out.

EILIF: Let her alone. Just give me some brandy.

THE SOLDIER: No.

THE CHAPLAIN: What shall we tell your mother?

EILIF: Tell her it was no different. Tell her it was the same. Oh, tell her nothing.

The soldiers take him away.

THE CHAPLAIN: I'll come with you, I'll . . .

EILIF: I don't need a priest!

THE CHAPLAIN: You don't know – yet. *He follows him.*

THE COOK, *calling after him*: I'll have to tell her, she'll want to see him!

THE CHAPLAIN: Better tell her nothing. Or maybe just that he was here, and he'll return, maybe tomorrow. Meantime I'll be back and can break the news. *He leaves quickly. The cook looks after him, shakes his head, then walks about uneasily. Finally, he approaches the wagon.*

THE COOK: Hello! Won't you come out? You want to sneak away from the peace, don't you? Well, so do I! I'm the Swedish Commander's cook, remember me? I was wondering if you've got anything to eat in there – while we're waiting for your mother. I wouldn't mind a bit of bacon – or even bread – just to pass the time. *He looks in.* She's got a blanket over her head. *The thunder of cannon.*

MOTHER COURAGE *runs in, out of breath, still carrying the goods*: Cook, the peace is over, the war's on again, has been for three days! I didn't get rid of this stuff after all, thank God! There's a shooting match in the town already – with the Lutherans. We must get away with the wagon. Pack, Kattrin! What's on *your* mind? Something the matter?

THE COOK: Nothing.

MOTHER COURAGE: But there is. I see it in your face.

THE COOK: Because the war's on again, most likely. May it last till tomorrow evening, so I can get something in my belly!

MOTHER COURAGE: You're not telling me.

THE COOK: Eilif was here. Only he had to go away again.

MOTHER COURAGE: He was here? Then we'll see him on the march. I'll be with our side this time. How'd he look?

THE COOK: The same.

MOTHER COURAGE: He'll *never* change. And the war couldn't get *him*, he's bright. Help me with the packing. *She starts it.* Did he tell you anything? Is he well in with the captain? Did he tell you about his heroic deeds?

THE COOK, *darkly*: He's done one of them again.

MOTHER COURAGE: Tell me about it later. *Kattrin appears.* Kattrin, the peace is over, we're on the move again. *To the cook*: What *is* the matter with you?

THE COOK: I'll enlist.

MOTHER COURAGE: A good idea. Where's the chaplain?

THE COOK: In the town. With Eilif.

MOTHER COURAGE: Stay with us a while, Lamb, I need a bit of help.

THE COOK: This matter of Yvette . . .

MOTHER COURAGE: Hasn't done you any harm at all in my eyes. Just the opposite. Where there's smoke, there's fire, they say. You'll come?

THE COOK: I may as well.

MOTHER COURAGE: The twelfth regiment's under way. Into harness with you! Maybe I'll see Eilif before the day is out, just think! That's what I like best. Well, it wasn't such a long peace, we can't grumble. Let's go!

The cook and Kattrin are in harness.

MOTHER COURAGE *sings*:

> From Ulm to Metz, past dome and steeple
> My wagon always moves ahead.
> The war can care for all its people
> So long as there is steel and lead.
> Though steel and lead are stout supporters
> A war needs human beings too.
> Report today to your headquarters!
> If it's to last, this war needs you!

9

THE GREAT WAR OF RELIGION HAS LASTED SIXTEEN YEARS AND
GERMANY HAS LOST HALF ITS INHABITANTS. THOSE WHO ARE
SPARED IN BATTLE DIE BY PLAGUE. OVER ONCE BLOOMING
COUNTRYSIDE HUNGER RAGES. TOWNS ARE BURNED DOWN.
WOLVES PROWL THE EMPTY STREETS. IN THE AUTUMN OF 1634
WE FIND MOTHER COURAGE IN THE FICHTELGEBIRGE NOT FAR
FROM THE ROAD THE SWEDISH ARMY IS TAKING. WINTER HAS
COME EARLY AND IS HARD. BUSINESS IS BAD. ONLY BEGGING
REMAINS. THE COOK RECEIVES A LETTER FROM UTRECHT AND
IS SENT PACKING.

In front of a Half-ruined Parsonage

*Early winter. A grey morning. Gusts of wind. Mother Courage and
the cook at the wagon in shabby clothes.*

THE COOK: There are no lights on. No one's up.

MOTHER COURAGE: But it's a parsonage. The parson'll have to
leave his feather bed and ring the bells. Then he'll have some
hot soup.

THE COOK: Where'll he get it from? The whole village is starving.

MOTHER COURAGE: The house is lived in. There was a dog
barking.

THE COOK: If the parson has anything, he'll stick to it.

MOTHER COURAGE: Maybe if we sang him something . . .

THE COOK: I've had enough. *Suddenly.* I didn't tell you, a letter
came from Utrecht My mother's died of cholera, the inn is
mine. There's the letter, if you don't believe me. I'll show it
to you, though my aunt's railing about me and my ups and
downs is none of your business.

MOTHER COURAGE, *reading*: Lamb, I'm tired of wandering, too.
I feel like a butcher's dog taking meat to my customers and
getting none myself. I've nothing more to sell and people
have nothing to pay with. In Saxony someone tried to saddle
me with a chestful of books in return for two eggs. And in
Württemberg they would have let me have their plough for
a bag of salt. Nothing grows any more, only thorn bushes.

In Pomerania I hear the villagers have been eating their younger children. Nuns have been caught committing robbery.

THE COOK: The world's dying out.

MOTHER COURAGE: Sometimes I see myself driving through hell with this wagon and selling brimstone. And sometimes I'm driving through heaven handing our provisions to wandering souls! If only we could find a place where there's no shooting, me and my children – what's left of 'em – we might rest a while.

THE COOK: We could open this inn together. Think about it, Courage. *My* mind's made up. With or without you, I'm leaving for Utrecht. And today too.

MOTHER COURAGE: I must talk to Kattrin, it's a little bit sudden, and I don't like to make my decisions in the cold on an empty stomach. *Kattrin emerges from the wagon.* Kattrin, I've something to tell you. The cook and I want to go to Utrecht, he's been left an inn. You'd be able to stay put and get to know some people. Many a man'd be prepared to take a girl with a position. Looks aren't everything. I wouldn't mind it. I get on well with the cook. I'll say this for him: he has a head for business. We'd be sure of our dinner, that would be all right, wouldn't it? You'd have your own bed, what do you think of *that*? In the long run, this is no life, on the road. You might be killed any time. You're eaten up with lice. And we must decide now, because otherwise we go north with the Swedes. They must be over there somewhere. *She points left.* I think we'll decide to go, Kattrin.

THE COOK: Anna, I must have a word with you alone.

MOTHER COURAGE: Go back inside, Kattrin. *Kattrin does so.*

THE COOK: I'm interrupting because there's a misunderstanding, Anna. I thought I wouldn't have to say it right out, but I see I must. If you're bringing *her*, it's all off. Do we understand each other?

Kattrin has her head out of the back of the wagon and is listening.

MOTHER COURAGE: You mean I leave Kattrin behind?

68

THE COOK: What do you think? There's no room in the inn, it isn't one of those places with three counters. If the two of us look lively we can earn a living, but three's too many. Let Kattrin keep your wagon.

MOTHER COURAGE: I was thinking we might find her a husband in Utrecht.

THE COOK: Don't make me laugh. With that scar? And old as she is? And dumb?

MOTHER COURAGE: Not so loud!

THE COOK: Loud or soft, what is, is. That's another reason I can't have her in the inn. Customers don't like having something like that always before their eyes. You can't blame them.

MOTHER COURAGE: Shut up. I told you not to talk so loud.

THE COOK: There's a light in the parsonage, we can sing now!

MOTHER COURAGE: Cook, how could she pull the wagon by herself? The war frightens her. She can't bear it. She has terrible dreams. I hear her groan at night, especially after battles. What she sees in her dreams I don't know. She suffers from sheer pity. The other day I found a hedgehog with her that we'd run over.

THE COOK: The inn's too small. *Calling*: Worthy Sir, menials, and all within! We now present the song of Solomon, Julius Caesar, and other great souls who came to no good, so you can see we're law-abiding folk too, and have a hard time getting by, especially in winter. *He sings*:

> You've heard of wise old Solomon
> You know his history.
> He thought so little of this earth
> He cursed the hour of his birth
> Declaring: all is vanity.
> How very wise was Solomon!
> But ere night came and day did go
> This fact was clear to everyone:
> It was his wisdom that had brought him low.
> Better for you if you have none.

69

For the virtues are dangerous in this world, as our fine song tells. You're better off without, you have a nice life, breakfast included – some good hot soup maybe . . . I'm an example of a man who's not had any, and I'd like some, I'm a soldier, but what good did my bravery do me in all those battles? None at all. I might just as well have wet my pants like a poltroon and stayed at home. For why?

> And Julius Caesar, who was brave
> You saw what came of him.
> He sat like God on an altar-piece
> And yet they tore him limb from limb
> While his prestige did still increase!
> 'Et tu, Brute, I am undone!'
> And ere night came and day did go
> This fact was clear to everyone:
> It was his bravery that brought him low
> Better for you if you have none.

Under his breath. They don't even look out. *Aloud.* Worthy Sir, menials, and all within! You should say, no, courage isn't the thing to fill a man's belly, try honesty, that should be worth a dinner, at any rate it must have *some* effect. Let's see.

> You all know honest Socrates
> Who always spoke the truth.
> They owed him thanks for that, you'd think
> Yet they put hemlock in his drink
> And swore that he was bad for youth.
> How honest was the people's son!
> But ere night came and day did go
> This fact was clear to everyone:
> It was his honesty that brought him low
> Better for you if you have none.

Yes, we're told to be unselfish and share what we have, but what if we have nothing? And those who do share it don't have an easy time either, for what's left when you've finished sharing? Unselfishness is a very rare virtue – it doesn't pay.

Unselfish Martin could not bear
His fellow creature's woes.
He met a beggar in the snows
And gave him half his cloak to wear:
So both of them fell down and froze.
What an unselfish paragon!
But ere night came and day did go
This fact was clear to everyone:
It was unselfishness that brought him low.
Better for you if you have none.

That's how it is with us. We're law-abiding folk, we keep to ourselves, don't steal, don't kill, don't burn the place down. And in this way we sink lower and lower and the song proves true and there's no soup going. And if we were different, if we were thieves and killers, maybe we could eat our fill! For virtues bring no reward, only vices. Such is the world, need it be so?

God's Ten Commandments we have kept
And acted as we should.
It has not done us any good.
O you who sit beside a fire
Please help us now: our need is dire!
Strict godliness we've always shown
But ere night came and day did go
This fact was clear to everyone:
It was our godliness that brought us low.
Better for you if you have none!

VOICE *from above*: You there! Come up! There's some soup here for you!

MOTHER COURAGE: Lamb, I couldn't swallow a thing. I don't say what you said is unreasonable, but was it your last word? We've always understood each other.

THE COOK: Yes, Anna. Think it over.

MOTHER COURAGE: There's nothing to think over. I'm not leaving her here.

THE COOK: You're going to be silly, but what can I do? I'm not inhuman, it's just that the inn's a small one. And now we must go up, or it'll be nothing doing here too, and we've been singing in the cold for nothing.

MOTHER COURAGE: I'll fetch Kattrin.

THE COOK: Better stick something in your pocket for her. If there are three of us, they'll get a shock. *Exeunt.*

Kattrin clambers out of the wagon with a bundle. She makes sure they are both gone. Then, on a wagon wheel, she lays out a skirt of her mother's and a pair of the cook's trousers side by side and easy to see. She has just finished, and has picked up her bundle, when Mother Courage returns.

MOTHER COURAGE, *with a plate of soup*: Kattrin! Stay where you are, Kattrin! Where do you think you're going with that bundle? *She examines the bundle.* She's packed her things. Were you listening? I told him there was nothing doing, he can *have* Utrecht and his lousy inn, what could we want with a lousy inn? *She sees the skirt and trousers.* Oh, you're a stupid girl, Kattrin, what if I'd seen that and you gone? *She takes hold of Kattrin who is trying to leave.* And don't think I've sent him packing on your account. It was the wagon. You can't part us, I'm too used to it, *you* didn't come into it, it was the wagon. Now we're leaving, and we'll put the cook's things here where he'll find 'em, the stupid man. *She clambers up and throws a couple of things down to go with the trousers.* There! He's sacked! The last man I'll take into *this* business! Now let's be going, you and me. Get into harness. This winter'll pass – like all the others.

They harness themselves to the wagon, turn it round, and start out. A gust of wind. Enter the cook, still chewing. He sees his things.

DURING THE WHOLE OF 1635 MOTHER COURAGE AND KATTRIN
PULL THE WAGON ALONG THE ROADS OF CENTRAL GERMANY IN
THE WAKE OF THE EVER MORE TATTERED ARMIES.

On the Highway

*Mother Courage and Kattrin are pulling the wagon. They come to
a prosperous farmhouse. Someone inside is singing.*

THE VOICE:

> In March a tree we planted
> To make the garden gay.
> In June we were enchanted:
> A lovely rose was blooming
> The balmy air perfuming!
> Blest of the gods are they
> Who have a garden gay!
> In June we were enchanted.
>
> When snow falls helter-skelter
> And loudly blows the storm
> Our farmhouse gives us shelter.
> The winter's in a hurry
> But we've no cause to worry.
> Cosy are we and warm
> Though loudly blows the storm
> Our farmhouse gives us shelter.

*Mother Courage and Kattrin have stopped to listen. Then they start
out again.*

II

JANUARY, 1636. CATHOLIC TROOPS THREATEN THE PROTES-
TANT TOWN OF HALLE. THE STONE BEGINS TO SPEAK. MOTHER
COURAGE LOSES HER DAUGHTER AND JOURNEYS ONWARDS
ALONE, THE WAR IS NOT YET NEAR ITS END.

*The wagon, very far gone now, stands near a farmhouse with a straw
roof. It is night. Out of the wood come a lieutenant and three soldiers
in full armour.*

THE LIEUTENANT: And there mustn't be a sound: If anyone
yells, cut him down.

THE FIRST SOLDIER: But we'll have to knock – if we want a
guide.

THE LIEUTENANT: Knocking's a natural noise, it's all right,
could be a cow hitting the wall of the cowshed.

*The soldiers knock at the farmhouse door. An old peasant woman
opens. A hand is clapped over her mouth. Two soldiers enter.*

A MAN'S VOICE: What is it?

The soldier brings out an old peasant and his scn.

THE LIEUTENANT, *pointing to the wagon on which Kattrin has
appeared*: There's one. *A soldier pulls her out.* Is this everybody that lives here?

THE PEASANTS, *alternating*: That's our son. And that's a girl
that can't talk. Her mother's in town buying up stocks because the shopkeepers are running away and selling cheap.
They're canteen people.

THE LIEUTENANT: I'm warning you. Keep quiet. One sound
and we'll crack you over the head with a pike. And I need
someone to show us the path to the town. *He points to the
young peasant.* You! Come here!

THE YOUNG PEASANT: I don't know any path!

THE SECOND SOLDIER, *grinning*: He don't know any path!

THE YOUNG PEASANT: I don't help Catholics.

74

THE LIEUTENANT, *to the second soldier*: Let him feel your pike in his side.

THE YOUNG PEASANT, *forced to his knees, the pike at his throat*: I'd rather die!

THE SECOND SOLDIER, *again mimicking*: He'd rather die!

THE FIRST SOLDIER: I know how to change his mind. *He walks over to the cowshed.* Two cows and a bull. Listen, you. If you aren't going to be reasonable, I'll sabre your cattle.

THE YOUNG PEASANT: Not the cattle!

THE PEASANT WOMAN, *weeping*: Spare the cattle, captain, or we'll starve!

THE LIEUTENANT: If he must be pigheaded!

THE FIRST SOLDIER: I think I'll start with the bull.

THE YOUNG PEASANT, *to the old one*: Do I have to? *The older one nods.* I'll do it.

THE PEASANT WOMAN: Thank you, thank you, captain, for sparing us, for ever and ever, Amen.

The old man stops her going on thanking him.

THE FIRST SOLDIER: I knew the bull came first all right!

Led by the young peasant, the lieutenant and the soldiers go on their way.

THE OLD PEASANT: I wish we knew what it was. Nothing good, I suppose.

THE PEASANT WOMAN: Maybe they're just scouts. What are you doing?

THE OLD PEASANT, *setting a ladder against the roof and climbing up*: I'm seeing if they're alone. *On the roof.* Things are moving – all over. I can see armour. And a cannon. There must be more than a regiment. God have mercy on the town and all within!

THE PEASANT WOMAN: Are there lights in the town?

THE OLD PEASANT: No, they're all asleep. *He climbs down.* There'll be an attack, and they'll all be slaughtered in their beds.

THE PEASANT WOMAN: The watchman'll give warning.

THE OLD PEASANT: They must have killed the watchman in the tower on the hill or he'd have sounded his horn before this.

THE PEASANT WOMAN: If there were more of us . . .

THE OLD PEASANT: But being that we're alone with that cripple . . .

THE PEASANT WOMAN: There's nothing we can do, is there?

THE OLD PEASANT: Nothing.

THE PEASANT WOMAN: We can't get down there. In the dark.

THE OLD PEASANT: The whole hillside's swarming with 'em.

THE PEASANT WOMAN: We could give a sign?

THE OLD PEASANT: And be cut down for it?

THE PEASANT WOMAN: No, there's nothing we can do. *To Kattrin*: Pray, poor thing, pray! There's nothing we can do to stop this bloodshed, so even if you can't talk, at least pray! He hears, if no one else does. I'll help you. *All kneel, Kattrin behind*. Our Father, which art in Heaven, hear our prayer, let not the town perish with all that lie therein asleep and fearing nothing. Wake them, that they rise and go to the walls and see the foe that comes with fire and sword in the night down the hill and across the fields. *Back to Kattrin*: God protect our mother and make the watchman not sleep but wake ere it's too late. And save our son-in-law too, O God, he's there with his four children, let them not perish, they're innocent, they know nothing – *To Kattrin, who groans* – one of them's not two years old, the eldest is seven. *Kattrin rises, troubled*. Heavenly Father, hear us, only Thou canst help us or we die, for we are weak and have no sword nor nothing; we cannot trust our own strength but only Thine, O Lord; we are in Thy hands, our cattle, our farm, and the town too, we're all in Thy hands, and the foe is nigh unto the walls with all his power.

Kattrin, unperceived, has crept off to the wagon, has taken something out of it, put it under her apron, and has climbed up the ladder to the roof.

Be mindful of the children in danger, especially the little ones, be mindful of the old folk who cannot move, and of all Christian souls, O Lord.

THE OLD PEASANT: And forgive us our trespasses as we forgive them that trespass against us. Amen.

Sitting on the roof, Kattrin takes a drum from under her apron and starts to beat it.

THE PEASANT WOMAN: Heavens, what's she doing?
THE OLD PEASANT: She's out of her mind!
THE PEASANT WOMAN: Get her down, quick!

The old peasant runs to the ladder but Kattrin pulls it up on the roof.

She'll get us in trouble.
THE OLD PEASANT: Stop it this minute, you silly cripple!
THE PEASANT WOMAN: The soldiers'll come!
THE OLD PEASANT, *looking for stones*: I'll stone you!
THE PEASANT WOMAN: Have you no pity, have you no heart? We have relations there too, four grandchildren, but there's nothing we can do. If they find us now, it's the end, they'll stab us to death!

Kattrin is staring into the far distance, towards the town. She goes on drumming.

THE PEASANT WOMAN, *to the peasant*: I told you not to let that riffraff in your farm. What do *they* care if we lose our cattle?
THE LIEUTENANT, *running back with soldiers and the young peasant*: I'll cut you all to bits!
THE PEASANT WOMAN: We're innocent, sir, there's nothing we can do. She did it, a stranger!
THE LIEUTENANT: Where's the ladder?
THE OLD PEASANT: On the roof.
THE LIEUTENANT, *calling*: Throw down the drum. I order you! *Kattrin goes on drumming.* You're all in this, but you won't live to tell the tale.
THE OLD PEASANT: They've been cutting down fir trees around here. If we bring a tall enough trunk we can knock her off the roof . . .
THE FIRST SOLDIER, *to the lieutenant*: I beg leave to make a suggestion. *He whispers something to the lieutenant, who nods.*

77

Listen, you! We have an idea – for your own good. Come down and go with us to the town. Show us your mother and we'll spare her.

Kattrin goes on drumming.

THE LIEUTENANT, *pushing him away*: She doesn't trust you, no wonder with your face. *He calls up to Kattrin*: Hey, you! Suppose I give you my word? I'm an officer, my word's my bond!

Kattrin drums harder.

Nothing is sacred to her.

THE YOUNG PEASANT: Sir, it's not just because of her mother!

THE FIRST SOLDIER: This can't go on, they'll hear it in the town as sure as hell.

THE LIEUTENANT: We must make another noise with something. Louder than that drum. What can we make a noise with?

THE FIRST SOLDIER: But we mustn't make a noise!

THE LIEUTENANT: A harmless noise, fool, a peacetime noise!

THE OLD PEASANT: I could start chopping wood.

THE LIEUTENANT: That's it! *The peasant brings his axe and chops away.* Chop! Chop harder! Chop for your life! *Kattrin has been listening, beating the drum less hard. Very upset, and peering around, she now goes on drumming.* It's not enough. *To the first soldier*: You chop too!

THE OLD PEASANT: I've only one axe. *He stops chopping.*

THE LIEUTENANT: We must set fire to the farm. Smoke her out.

THE OLD PEASANT: That's no good, Captain. When they see fire from the town, they'll know everything.

During the drumming Kattrin has been listening again. Now she laughs.

THE LIEUTENANT: She's laughing at us, that's too much, I'll have her guts if it's the last thing I do. Bring a musket!

Two soldiers off. Kattrin goes on drumming.

THE PEASANT WOMAN: I have it, Captain. That's their wagon

over there, Captain. If we smash that, she'll stop. It's all they have, Captain.

THE LIEUTENANT, *to the young peasant*: Smash it! *Calling*: If you don't stop that noise, we'll smash your wagon!

The young peasant deals the wagon a couple of feeble blows with a board.

THE PEASANT WOMAN, *to Kattrin*: Stop, you little beast!

Kattrin stares at the wagon and pauses. Noises of distress come out of her. But she goes on drumming.

THE LIEUTENANT: Where are those sons of bitches with that gun?

THE FIRST SOLDIER: They can't have heard anything in the town or we'd hear their cannon.

THE LIEUTENANT, *calling*: They don't hear. And now we're going to shoot you. I'll give you one more chance: throw down that drum!

THE YOUNG PEASANT, *dropping the board, screaming to Kattrin*: Don't stop now! Or they're all done for. Go on, go on, go on . . .

The soldier knocks him down and beats him with his pike. Kattrin starts crying but goes on drumming.

THE PEASANT WOMAN: Not in the back, you're killing him!

The soldiers arrive with the musket.

THE SECOND SOLDIER: The Colonel's foaming at the mouth. We'll be courtmartialled.

THE LIEUTENANT: Set it up! Set it up! *Calling while the musket is set up on forks*: Once and for all: stop that drumming!

Still crying, Kattrin is drumming as hard as she can.

Fire!

The soldiers fire. Kattrin is hit. She gives the drum another feeble beat or two, then slowly collapses.

THE LIEUTENANT: That's an end to the noise.

But the last beats of the drum are lost in the din of cannon from the town. Mingled with the thunder of cannon, alarm-bells are heard in the distance.

THE FIRST SOLDIER: She did it.

12

Towards morning. The drums and pipes of troops on the march, receding. In front of the wagon Mother Courage sits by Kattrin's body. The peasants of the last scene are standing near.

THE PEASANTS: You must leave, woman. There's only one regiment to go. You can never get away by yourself.

MOTHER COURAGE: Maybe she's fallen asleep.

She sings:

> Lullay, lullay, what's that in the hay?
> The neighbour's babes cry but mine are gay.
> The neighbour's babes are dressed in dirt:
> Your silks were cut from an angel's skirt.
> They are all starving: you have a cake;
> If it's too stale, you need but speak.
> Lullay, lullay, what's rustling there?
> One lad fell in Poland. The other is where?

You shouldn't have told her about the children.

THE PEASANTS: If you hadn't gone off to the town to get your cut, maybe it wouldn't have happened.

MOTHER COURAGE: She's asleep now.

THE PEASANTS: She's not asleep, it's time you realized. She's gone. You must get away. There are wolves in these parts. And the bandits are worse.

MOTHER COURAGE: That's right.

She goes and fetches a cloth from the wagon to cover up the body.

THE PEASANT WOMAN: Have you no one now? Someone you can go to?

MOTHER COURAGE: There's one. My Eilif.

THE PEASANT, *while Mother Courage covers the body*: Find him then. Leave *her* to us. We'll give her a proper burial. You needn't worry.

MOTHER COURAGE: Here's money for the expenses.

She pays the peasant. The peasant and his son shake her hand and carry Kattrin away.

THE PEASANT WOMAN, *also taking her hand, and bowing, as she goes away*: Hurry!

MOTHER COURAGE, *harnessing herself to the wagon*: I hope I can pull the wagon by myself. Yes, I'll manage, there's not much in it now. I must start up again in business.

Another regiment passes at the rear with pipe and drum.

MOTHER COURAGE *starts pulling the wagon*: Hey! Take me with you!

Soldiers are heard singing:

Foldback

> Dangers, surprises, devastations –
> The war takes hold and will not quit.
> But though it last three generations
> We shall get nothing out of it.
> Starvation, filth, and cold enslave us.
> The army robs us of our pay.
> Only a miracle can save us
> And miracles have had their day.
> Christians, awake! The winter's gone!
> The snows depart. The dead sleep on.
> And though you may not long survive
> Get out of bed and look alive!

METHUEN'S MODERN PLAYS

Edited by John Cullen and Geoffrey Strachan